Kingdom and Culture

*God's Fivefold Strategy for
Changing Our World*

Kingdom and Culture

Cover Design   Graham Alder

Contact Details   gb@elimmetro.com

ISBN   978-1-907929-08-3

Life Publications

Endorsements

* *Geoff's book is full of principles to bring change to our society. He takes us on a journey into how kingdoms work and function. He then takes us deeper into how kingdoms are set up in our culture. Finally, he gives lots of practical steps on how believers in a loving God can effect change to the cultures and the kingdoms of this world. A passionate call for this very possible revolution.*

Steve Long, Senior Pastor, Catch the Fire Toronto
(Catch the Fire Toronto hosted the "Toronto Blessing", a revival which attracted more than four million people. The church today has multiple venues in Toronto and has a global impact through schools, missions and churches around the world.)

* *Geoff has set out for us his view of the Kingdom of God and the rights and responsibilities we have within it. Rather than simply diagnosing the demise of a degenerating culture, he offers an antidote in the form of the church. A well-researched and challenging read.*

Rev John Glass, General Superintendent, Elim Pentecostal Churches

* *It has been my privilege to work closely with Geoff for almost a decade and I have always been impressed by his integrity and passion for the King and His Kingdom. In this thoughtful and thought provoking book Geoff shares practical insights into the Kingdom of God that will actually work in the lives of ordinary people like* *me. He deals with current thinking in a relevant and accessible way and the result is a very readable book full of scripture and common sense.*

Rev David Campbell, Regional Leader, Elim Pentecostal Churches

*

Geoff studied authority during his career in the British Army and has experienced being both "under" and "in" authority in the business world and also in the church. He throws great light on the authority of the believer and the believer's role within the walls of the "Seven Mountains" that shape the cultures in which we all live. What an eye opener!

This book will be very useful to both leaders and ordinary believers alike. This is must read material!

Rev (Major rtd) Sam Larbie, Senior Pastor, Elim Camberwell, London

Dedication

To the Father Who loves us
To the Son Who saves us
To the Spirit Who empowers us

Kingdom and Culture

Contents

Part Three

Preface

What is the Kingdom of God? How much of the Kingdom of God can we experience today? How does the Kingdom of God relate to the ever increasing secularisation of society and culture?

These are questions as old as the scriptures themselves but which seem to be so current and as relevant to us as we enter a new and exciting decade in the destiny of humanity.

Jesus Himself, when asked by His disciples to give them instruction as to how they should pray, answered them with these words.

> *Thy Kingdom come; Thy will be done on earth*
> *as it is in Heaven"*

The question then arises as to what Christians might expect to experience in their day to day lives of the Kingdom of God for themselves and for their families. To what extent can we expect the will of God to be done on earth before the glorious and triumphant return of the Lord Jesus Christ in glory?

The answers to these questions, will determine the hope and expectation for those who seek to live by, and experience, the reality of the Christian faith as they face the challenges of the modern world.

These are exciting days indeed with several books currently available challenging Christians to take dominion over the "Seven Mountains of Culture" and thereby heralding in the Kingdom rule of God.

Certainly there needs to be a loud and passionate cry to the church not only to "Awaken" to the ungodliness that pervades the earthly cultures but also to "Arise and Shine" and take whatever action it can in order to see the *"Kingdom come and God's will done on earth as it is in Heaven!"* One thing we cannot do is merely sit in our buildings and sing triumphalist songs of victory, however inspiring they may be, without living out and experiencing the reality of what the songs profess.

This book seeks to address these issues in an easy to follow, step by step, logical progression. It is not intended to be a theological treatise, but it does contain sound theology and a firm Biblical foundation. It is meant to appeal to all who have enquiring minds and passionate hearts, and who want to taste the reality of God in our day.

Having established some understanding on the principles and precepts concerning the Kingdom it then endeavours to give some clear guidelines that will both inspire and empower the reader to be that person who is freed from the shackles of history and released to fulfil the destiny of the call of God in this age.

Finally, we shall discover God's Fivefold Strategic Plan for changing our world. This is not "triumphalism" nor "dominionism" but rather a Biblically based strategy that draws together the different strands of Christian activity, so that together we make the difference!

Introduction

It was sometime in 2009 that I was first introduced to the teaching that is now known as the "Seven Mountains" and "The Elijah Revolution". It resonated with a deep longing in the core of my passion to see Christians come of age and stand up to be the powerful and prophetic people of destiny and influence that God intended for His New Testament church. In fact in my first book, which has now been republished under the title of *Adoption and Destiny,*[1] I encouraged Christians to rise up in their new identity as sons and daughters of the Living God and to realise that they are called, not only to "be different" but also to "make a difference". The challenge before us however is the extent of that difference and what might realistically be expected as we rise up in faith, filled with and empowered by the Holy Spirit to fulfil the Great Commission and to make disciples of all nations.

If we are to take seriously the last words of Jesus on earth then we shall need to understand the relationship between the Kingdom of Heaven and the kingdoms of this world. We shall need to clearly understand the glorious truths of what it means to be "*rescued from the dominion of darkness and brought into the kingdom of the Son He loves*".[2]

---

[1] First published in 2009 under the title *Adoption, Sonship, and the Family Business*. (Life Publications ISBN978095619963-8)

[2] Colossians 1:13 NIV

The Bible declares that the believer in Christ is *'raised up with Christ and seated with him in the heavenly realms in Christ Jesus'.* A few verses earlier in Ephesians we read a description of those heavenly realms.

> *I pray also that the eyes of your heart may be enlightened in order that you may know the hope to which he has called you, the riches of his glorious inheritance in the saints, and his incomparably great power for us who believe. That power is like the working of his mighty strength, which he exerted in Christ when he raised him from the dead and seated him at his right hand in the heavenly realms, far above all rule and authority, power and dominion, and every title that can be given, not only in the present age but also in the one to come. And God placed all things under his feet and appointed him to be head over everything for the church, which is his body, the fullness of him who fills everything in every way.*

> Ephesians 1:18-23

This is an awesome passage of Scripture for us to grasp and to realise the positional authority that the church has been awarded through being seated in these heavenly realms in Christ Jesus.

In the pages that follow we shall examine what it means for the believer to be in the Kingdom of God and how that kingdom authority, dominion and influence can be exercised in relationship to the society and the cultures of the people groups among which we live and work.

Introduction

If Christians fail to grasp both the extent, and the limitations, of their kingdom authority and dominion, then we shall fail to fulfil our destiny and our calling.

Firstly, we shall fail to stand up and exercise the spiritual authority that has been invested in the believer in this age and therefore, by default, permit the spiritual powers of darkness to rule where in fact they should be vanquished.

Secondly, if we fail to appreciate the God given parameters in which we can exercise Kingdom dominion, we shall be attempting activities that we are not empowered for, nor authorised to engage in, thus inviting defeat, disappointment, disillusionment and despair.

Success and victory are assured when carrying out God's plans, in God's time and with God's authority. A brief comparison of two Old Testament events will make the point.

Perhaps one of the most famous victories of the great Old Testament leader of God's people, Joshua, was at the battle of Jericho.

> *Now Jericho was tightly shut up because of the Israelites. No one went out and no one came in. Then the LORD said to Joshua, "See, I have delivered Jericho into your hands, along with its king and its fighting men. March around the city once with all the armed men. Do this for six days. Have seven priests carry trumpets of rams' horns in front of the ark. On the seventh day, march around the city seven times, with the priests blowing the trumpets. When you hear them sound a long blast on the trumpets, have all the people give a loud shout; then the wall of the city will collapse and the people will go up, every man straight in."*
>
> Joshua 6:1-5

The rest, as they say, is history. Because Joshua obeyed the commands of the Lord the victory was assured. Not so however during the next episode in Joshua's leadership of Israel.

After the complete rout of Jericho, Joshua decided that he should send out soldiers to defeat the town of Ai. The first problem with that decision was that he made it on his own. Perhaps the great victory at Jericho had caused him to be proud, perhaps even presumptuous. In his decision to attack Ai he did not consult the God who had previously promised success. That promise to Joshua of ongoing success was, however, conditional upon obedience to, and dependence upon the God who had commissioned him to lead his people.

> *Be strong and courageous, because you will lead these people to inherit the land I swore to their forefathers to give them. Be strong and very courageous. Be careful to obey all the law my servant Moses gave you; do not turn from it to the right or to the left, that you may be successful wherever you go. Do not let this Book of the Law depart from your mouth; meditate on it day and night, so that you may be careful to do everything written in it. Then you will be prosperous and successful. Have I not commanded you? Be strong and courageous. Do not be terrified; do not be discouraged, for the LORD your God will be with you wherever you go.*
>
> *Joshua 1:6-9*

The second problem that was to lead to defeat at Ai was unknown to Joshua. The problem was that not only was there presumption in the leadership, but there was also disobedience in the camp. God had commanded that there should be no spoils of victory taken from Jericho but this command was disobeyed by just one individual.

> *But the Israelites acted unfaithfully in regard to the devoted things; Achan son of Carmi, the son of Zimri, the son of Zerah, of the tribe of Judah, took some of them. So the LORD's anger burned against Israel.*
>
> Joshua 7:1

The consequences of these two mistakes is described very clearly,

> *Now Joshua sent men from Jericho to Ai, which is near Beth Aven to the east of Bethel, and told them, "Go up and spy out the region." So the men went up and spied out Ai. When they returned to Joshua, they said, "Not all the people will have to go up against Ai. Send two or three thousand men to take it and do not weary all the people, for only a few men are there." So about three thousand men went up; but they were routed by the men of Ai, who killed about thirty-six of them. They chased the Israelites from the city gate as far as the stone quarries and struck them down on the slopes. At this the hearts of the people melted and became like water.*
>
> Joshua 7:2-5

If we wish to see success, it is vital we understand that any authority given by God is on God's terms. When considering the relationship of the Kingdom of God to the cultures of the world it is important that we understand the principles of warfare and the rules of engagement.

Part One

Kingdom and Culture

1

The Principle
of the Kingdom

As I embark on this first chapter I am spending just a few days near Evesham in a very beautiful part of the United Kingdom. I can see through the windows the rolling hills, the resplendent trees as they display their autumnal glory and the array of agricultural endeavour as the recently ploughed fields herald their preparation for the next season.

How different to the dismay in the ghettos of so many of our cities and the impending gloom of the severe austerity measures imposed upon the nation by the current coalition government in the hope of bringing forth some sort of economic revival.

The reality is that although the governmental authority may be exactly the same, the personal experience of individuals can be extremely varied. This variation is due to such random factors as place of birth, family heritage, regional prosperity, financial privilege, ethnic origin, education and many others.

The United Kingdom is comprised of four clearly identifiable countries, England, Northern Ireland, Scotland and Wales.

Each of these historically separate identities have been united under the one Sovereign and the one Rule of Law. This Rule of Law is administered by the government in the Houses of Parliament. This system is known as a "Constitutional Monarchy".

A Constitutional Monarchy is a form of government in which the monarch acts as the head of state within the limitations of a written or unwritten constitution. The process of government is carried out by a parliamentary system with an elected prime minister. That election may be directly by the people or indirectly through the process of party leadership. The system works reasonably well and has been the prototype of many emerging nations of the world. However it is not a good example of what the bible teaches about the Kingdom of God.

Most western nations of the world operate in some form of "democracy" whereby the rulership and the government are determined by a majority vote of the citizens of that nation. The systems may vary in detail but the overarching principle is one of democratic government. Democracy has as one of its core values the "rights" of the individual and the vulnerability of the elected government to the "ballot box".

The benefit of such democratic forms of government is that they prevent the abuses of tyrannical dictatorships and the abuse of human rights that are possible under extreme dictatorships or absolute monarchs.

The danger for the western world however, in understanding the role of the Kingdom of God, is that western democratically inclined thinking has induced values that tend towards the absolute rights of the individual rather than the absolute rights of the monarch.

It may not seem "politically correct" to use such terms for the Kingdom of God but in reality the Kingdom of God is an

'Absolute Monarchy'. However, unlike most earthly absolute monarchies which are led by people with human frailties, God is perfect. We can also add a very important word that describes the monarch in the Kingdom of God. That important word is "Benevolent". In truth then the Kingdom of God must be considered in these terms as a "Benevolent Absolute Monarchy" and our western democratically orientated thinking must be adjusted if we are to really understand the significance of the difference.

There would be some benefit to be gained at this point from briefly stating the difference between what is "reign" and what is "realm". It will help in later chapters when the relationship between the Kingdom of God and the culture of the world is considered.

Reign

The word "reign" means to exercise rule and authority. The brothers of the dreamer Joseph knew well what this meant.

> *Joseph had a dream, and when he told it to his brothers, they hated him all the more. He said to them, "Listen to this dream I had: We were binding sheaves of grain out in the field when suddenly my sheaf rose and stood upright, while your sheaves gathered around mine and bowed down to it."*
>
> *His brothers said to him, "Do you intend to reign over us? Will you actually rule us?" And they hated him all the more because of his dream and what he had said.*
>
> *Genesis 37:5-8*

To reign is to have power and authority over others to the extent that they are accountable and subordinate in their position. It is the act of ruling.

Realm

On the other hand "realm" describes that which is ruled over. It can be a physical geographical area, it can be a people group, and it can also be spiritual powers. Another word with a similar meaning is "domain", which means that area where the ruler has "dominion".

2

The Character
of the Kingdom

The term Benevolent Absolute Monarchy is somewhat awkward but it does give some insight into the nature and the character of the King. The Bible is unambiguous in declaring that Jesus Christ is *"Lord of lords and King of kings"*.[3] There is no name that is above His name and no authority that is above His authority. When encouraging the faithful in Ephesus the apostle Paul wrote these words:

> *I pray also that the eyes of your heart may be enlightened in order that you may know the hope to which he has called you, the riches of his glorious inheritance in the saints, and his incomparably great power for us who believe. That power is like the working of his mighty strength, which he exerted in Christ when he raised him from the dead and seated him at his right hand in the heavenly realms, far above all rule and authority, power and dominion, and*

---

[3] Revelation 17:14 and Revelation 19:16

every title that can be given, not only in the present age but also in the one to come. And God placed all things under his feet and appointed him to be head over everything for the church, which is his body, the fullness of him who fills everything in every way.

Ephesians 1:18-23

This leaves us in no doubt about the absolute authority that is given to the sovereign in the Kingdom of God. With such absolute power and authority it is important for us to know the character of such a person if we are to be willing to submit to His rulership and government. Let us therefore take a look at some of the character traits of God.

God is Love

How comforting and reassuring it is therefore to know that this one almighty authority is not only governed by a principle of love, but is in fact the personification of love and all that it entails.

God is love. This is how God showed his love among us: He sent his one and only Son into the world that we might live through him. This is love: not that we loved God, but that he loved us and sent his Son as an atoning sacrifice for our sins.

1 John 4:7-10

It is so reassuring to fully appreciate that everything God is and everything that God does is from a position of love. It is not as if love is something God does as a choice, but rather being in "essence" love personified, all He ever does is contained within the parameters of His being. This type of love is known in the original Greek as *"agape"* love.

Agape Love

Here we have the very core of the Christian message. This is a love that has a genuine concern for the recipient irrespective of their own worthiness or attractiveness. It is a love that gives without thought or expectation of reciprocation in any form. It is a love that is selfless and a love that is given from a heart of compassion.

The practical outworking of this love is seen in 1 Corinthians 13 where the Apostle Paul encourages the Christians at Corinth to love each other with the same love that God in Christ loved us.

> *Love is patient, love is kind. It does not envy, it does not boast, it is not proud. It is not rude, it is not self-seeking, it is not easily angered, it keeps no record of wrongs. Love does not delight in evil but rejoices with the truth. It always protects, always trusts, always hopes, always perseveres. Love never fails.*
>
> *1 Corinthians 13:1-8*

It is important for us to appreciate that the Kingdom of God is governed by a sovereign whose actions emanate from the very essence of unconditional love. We cannot earn this love and therefore we cannot be disqualified to receive it. It has nothing to do with us, but all to do with God.

It is a love that initiates rather than responds. Perhaps one of the most well known verses in the Bible gives us an insight into God's motivation.

Kingdom and Culture

For God so loved the world that he gave his one and only Son, that whoever believes in him shall not perish but have eternal life. For God did not send his Son into the world to condemn the world, but to save the world through him.

John 3:16

The motivation of God, who exists above and beyond all others, is that of love. He took the initiative when mankind was lost in sin and beyond his own ability to save himself. God did not condemn man to the eternal consequences of his own mistakes but gave him a way of escape through faith in Christ Jesus. How wonderful to know that even in our rebellion God's actions were those of love.

You see, at just the right time, when we were still powerless, Christ died for the ungodly. Very rarely will anyone die for a righteous man, though for a good man someone might possibly dare to die. But God demonstrates his own love for us in this: While we were still sinners, Christ died for us.

Romans 5:6-8

This love is not passive but proactive. It takes the initiative to meet the needs of those who are the objects of this love. How wonderful to know that in the Kingdom of God we can find security within the realms of this perfect love. Knowing this will give us greater freedom than all the democratic fancies of human reasoning. Rather than bringing fear of oppression, it will release us into a confidence of our destiny as citizens of the Kingdom of God.

There is no fear in love. But perfect love drives out fear, because fear has to do with punishment.

1 John 4:18

There need be no fear in submitting our lives to God because we are loved with a perfect love that has freed us from the guilt of our sin through the atoning sacrifice of Jesus. Having been freed from the guilt we are also freed from the punishment.

In Jesus, all the Messianic prophecies were fulfilled. Therefore the passage in the fifty third chapter of Isaiah is also fulfilled and this deals with the release of punishment through the sacrifice of Jesus.

Surely he took up our infirmities and carried our sorrows, yet we considered him stricken by God, smitten by him, and afflicted. But he was pierced for our transgressions, he was crushed for our iniquities; the punishment that brought us peace was upon him, and by his wounds we are healed. We all, like sheep, have gone astray, each of us has turned to his own way; and the LORD has laid on him the iniquity of us all.

Isaiah 53:4-6

With such fulfilment through God's love where is the room for fear?

Kingdom and Culture

3

The Constitution
of the Kingdom

The aim of the constitution of a country, whatever the type of government, is to set the parameters in which government can take place. It sets out the Rule of Law by which citizens are governed and by which law and order is established. It also places on record the rights and responsibilities of all citizens.

The constitution of the Kingdom of God is contained in the Word of God, the Bible. Both the Old Testament and the New Testaments give divine instructions as to how life should be lived in the Kingdom of God. The Ten Commandments given to Moses[4] by Almighty God are clearly instructions for life in the Kingdom as indeed is the Olivet discourse of our Lord Jesus known as the Sermon on the Mount.[5]

The reply that Jesus gave to Satan during His temptation in the wilderness gives us a clear pointer to the responsibilities we have to the constitution of the Kingdom contained in Scripture.

---

[4] Exodus 20:1- 17

[5] Matthew chapters 5;6;7

Then Jesus was led by the Spirit into the desert to be tempted by the devil. After fasting forty days and forty nights, he was hungry. The tempter came to him and said, "If you are the Son of God, tell these stones to become bread." Jesus answered, "It is written: `Man does not live on bread alone, but on every word that comes from the mouth of God.' "Then the devil took him to the holy city and had him stand on the highest point of the temple. "If you are the Son of God," he said, "throw yourself down. For it is written "'He will command his angels concerning you, and they will lift you up in their hands, so that you will not strike your foot against a stone.' " Jesus answered him, "It is also written: `Do not put the Lord your God to the test.' "

Again, the devil took him to a very high mountain and showed him all the kingdoms of the world and their splendour. "All this I will give you," he said, "if you will bow down and worship me." Jesus said to him, "Away from me, Satan! For it is written: `Worship the Lord your God, and serve him only.' " Then the devil left him, and angels came and attended him.

Matthew 4:1-11

Jesus used the authority of Scripture as a counter to the temptations of Satan. Jesus used Scripture in this way because He understood it as having final authority to which Satan and man must submit.

It is not for us here to examine in detail all that the scriptures declare concerning the "constitution" of the Kingdom of God, but merely to establish that the Kingdom of God does have a written constitution to which its citizens are subject. However Psalm 19 does give us a brief insight into the benefits of living by them.

> *The law of the LORD is perfect, reviving the soul. The statutes of the LORD are trustworthy, making wise the simple. The precepts of the LORD are right, giving joy to the heart. The commands of the LORD are radiant, giving light to the eyes.*
>
> *The fear of the LORD is pure, enduring forever. The ordinances of the LORD are sure and altogether righteous. They are more precious than gold, than much pure gold. They are sweeter than honey, than honey from the comb. By them is your servant warned; in keeping them there is great reward.*
>
> Psalm 19:7-11

Access to the Kingdom

Although this subject will be covered later it would be helpful in these initial stages to establish the "rite of entry" into the Kingdom of God. Certainly we do not automatically enter the Kingdom of God at birth as some think, even though we may be born into what is known as a "Christian" country. Even the term "Christian" country is somewhat questionable in this present age.

We do not enter the Kingdom of God through parental faith, nor through such religious activities as dedication and infant baptism. There is only one access point through which we can enter the Kingdom of God and that is through personal faith in the Lord Jesus Christ as the Lamb of God who takes away the sin of the world.

Nicodemus was a leading Pharisee who asked Jesus about entry into God's Kingdom. Jesus answered by saying that in order to see and to enter the Kingdom of God a person must be, in His terms, "born again". How sad then that this most wonderful and poignant term has in so many ways been devalued by the media and others to describe some stylised caricature of a way out form of religion. It is indeed central to our understanding of how a person can enter the Kingdom of God.

This will be considered later in examining the "Extent of the Kingdom". For now let the words of Jesus confirm the importance of being "born again".

> *Now there was a man of the Pharisees named Nicodemus, a member of the Jewish ruling council. He came to Jesus at night and said, "Rabbi, we know you are a teacher who has come from God. For no one could perform the miraculous signs you are doing if God were not with him." In reply Jesus declared, "I tell you the truth, no one can see the kingdom of God unless he is born again."*
>
> *"How can a man be born when he is old?" Nicodemus asked. "Surely he cannot enter a second time into his mother's womb to be born!" Jesus answered, "I tell you the truth, no one can enter the kingdom of God unless he is born of water and the Spirit. Flesh gives birth to flesh, but the Spirit gives birth to spirit. You should*

> *not be surprised at my saying, 'You must be*
> *born again.'"*
>
> John 3:1-6

It is only through a spiritual rebirth that a person can gain access into the Kingdom of God and be delivered from the dominion of darkness in which the current state of fallen humanity exists.

> *For he has rescued us from the dominion of*
> *darkness and brought us into the kingdom of the*
> *Son he loves, in whom we have redemption, the*
> *forgiveness of sins.*
>
> Colossians 1:13

Please notice here that the principle of the Kingdom is not only some future realm but a present reality. It is not some eschatological proposition but something that can be experienced by the believer in the here and now.

The Primacy of the Kingdom

There are some things in life that are more important than others. Some things that are preferences and some that are priorities. There are some things that are absolutely essential and which take the focus of our attention like nothing else. Imagine then, the importance that should be attached to what Jesus says that we should seek above all else. Nothing else is as important and nothing else should prevent the primacy of the Kingdom of God in our lives.

In the Olivet discourse (Sermon on the Mount) Jesus does not say that the things of this world are not important. He does not say that we do not need clothing or food. However He does say that our searching for these natural requirements should take second place to the absolute priority of seeking first the Kingdom.

> *"No one can serve two masters. Either he will hate the one and love the other, or he will be devoted to the one and despise the other. You cannot serve both God and Money.*
>
> *"Therefore I tell you, do not worry about your life, what you will eat or drink; or about your body, what you will wear. Is not life more important than food, and the body more important than clothes? Look at the birds of the air; they do not sow or reap or store away in barns, and yet your heavenly Father feeds them. Are you not much more valuable than they? Who of you by worrying can add a single hour to his life?*
>
> *"And why do you worry about clothes? See how the lilies of the field grow. They do not labour or spin. Yet I tell you that not even Solomon in all his splendour was dressed like one of these. If that is how God clothes the grass of the field, which is here today and tomorrow is thrown into the fire, will he not much more clothe you, O you of little faith? So do not worry, saying, `What shall we eat?' or `What shall we drink?' or `What shall we wear?' For the pagans run after all these things, and your heavenly Father knows that you need them. But seek first his kingdom and his righteousness, and all these things will be given to you as well.*

> Matthew 6:24-33

The Constitution of the Kingdom

Jesus Himself said that the most important activity of man was to seek first the Kingdom of God and the righteousness that it embodies. If this becomes the prime purpose of our lives then we will find everything else within the natural realm taken care of by our Heavenly Father.

Many people find that they spend so much of their lives chasing after the things of this world that they have little time left for seeking after God. Is it any wonder therefore that there is so much unfulfilment in our world, so much unrighteousness in our world, so much pain and anxiety?

The apostle Paul when writing to the believers in Rome encouraged them concerning the Kingdom of God. He stressed the primacy of the spiritual Kingdom over the natural and reminded them that the benefits of such a Kingdom were to be life fulfilling.

> *For the kingdom of God is not a matter of eating and drinking, but of righteousness, peace and joy in the Holy Spirit, because anyone who serves Christ in this way is pleasing to God and approved by men.*

> Romans 14:17

Kingdom and Culture

4

Present Reality
and Future Promise

As we consider the apparent "tension" between the present reality and the future promise of the Kingdom of God we must appreciate that this subject has been a source of theological debate for as long as theology has been debated! However we should not be deterred from seeking some understanding of the different positions but rather consider what the Bible itself declares the truth to be.

In fact the Bible does present us with some very complex information about the Kingdom of God some of which may seem to provide more questions than answers. Fear not, dear reader, we shall survive! It is our understanding of this "tension" that will shape our thinking and actions as we respond to the commission of Jesus to the church to "*make disciples of all nations*".

The Present Reality

The fact that the Kingdom of God is a present reality is confirmed by many Scriptures. In several places the Kingdom of God is referred to as an "eternal" kingdom. If it is eternal then by definition it has no beginning and no end. It is ever existent and ever the same. There has never been a time when the Kingdom was not and therefore there will never be a time when the Kingdom will cease to exist.

I will exalt you, my God the King; I will praise your name for ever and ever. Every day I will praise you. I will extol your name for ever and ever. Great is the LORD and most worthy of praise; his greatness no one can fathom. One generation will commend your works to another; they will tell of your mighty acts. They will speak of the glorious splendour of your majesty, and I will meditate on your wonderful works. They will tell of the power of your awesome works, and I will proclaim your great deeds. They will celebrate your abundant goodness and joyfully sing of your righteousness.

The LORD is gracious and compassionate, slow to anger and rich in love. The LORD is good to all; he has compassion on all he has made. All you have made will praise you, O LORD; your saints will extol you.

They will tell of the glory of your kingdom and speak of your might, so that all men may know of your mighty acts and the glorious splendour of your kingdom. Your kingdom is an everlasting kingdom, and your dominion endures through all generations.

Psalm 145:1-13

Because the Kingdom of God is eternal it existed before the creation of the world and will continue forward into eternity.

At this point it must be understood that Scripture also declares the Kingdom of God, not only to be eternal, but is "at hand" and also "to come". It is within this conundrum that we will find the role of the church in fulfilling the Great Commission.

Some verses to consider are as follows:

But if I drive out demons by the Spirit of God, then the kingdom of God has come upon you.

Matthew 12:28

This verse clearly indicates that the Kingdom of God is present and operates within the lives of individuals. On the other hand we can see from other verses that the Kingdom of God is yet a promise of some future event.

I declare to you, brothers, that flesh and blood cannot inherit the kingdom of God, nor does the perishable inherit the imperishable.

1 Corinthians 15:50

In the gospel of Matthew we read that the Kingdom of God is something that we must enter in the present.

Jesus said to them, "I tell you the truth, the tax collectors and the prostitutes are entering the kingdom of God ahead of you. For John came to you to show you the way of righteousness, and

39

*you did not believe him, but the tax collectors
and the prostitutes did. And even after you saw
this, you did not repent and believe him.*

Matthew 21:31-32

In this we learn from Jesus that the prostitutes and tax collectors "are" entering into the Kingdom of God now. There is also an inference by Jesus that the way into the Kingdom is through repentance and faith. This truth we shall establish later.

Variations on a Theme

It is very interesting to take an overview of some of the various interpretations that have been held in the past, and indeed continue today, over the Kingdom of God.

Although it is not the intention here to plumb the depths of theological arguments, it will be of great assistance to our understanding of the relationship between the Kingdom of God and the Cultures of this world.

The Kingdom is Now

The first interpretation that we will consider is one that states that the Kingdom is now a present reality on the earth and was fully realised in the mission and the ministry of Jesus. This view claims that the Kingdom came with Jesus and exists today among those who will submit their lives to God and through whom the Holy Spirit produces such fruit as righteousness, peace and joy. This theory was espoused by C.H. Dodd and was based upon such Scriptures as those listed below.

*But if I drive out demons by the Spirit of God,
then the kingdom of God has come upon you.*

Matthew 12:28

40

For the kingdom of God is not a matter of eating and drinking, but of righteousness, peace and joy in the Holy Spirit.

Romans 14:17

For he has rescued us from the dominion of darkness and brought us into the kingdom of the Son he loves, in whom we have redemption, the forgiveness of sins.

Colossians 1:13-14

The Kingdom is Future

The second view states that the Kingdom of God is not for this time but is restricted to a future blessing that is to be given only to God's people at the Second Coming of Jesus Christ. It argues that the current state of human existence will cease and be replaced by a new heavenly order. One of the past theologians who supported this theory was Albert Schweitzer. His view was gained from his understanding of the following Scriptures.

I declare to you, brothers, that flesh and blood cannot inherit the kingdom of God, nor does the perishable inherit the imperishable.

1 Corinthians 15:50

I say to you that many will come from the east and the west, and will take their places at the feast with Abraham, Isaac and Jacob in the kingdom of heaven.

Matthew 8:11

...and you will receive a rich welcome into the eternal kingdom of our Lord and Saviour Jesus Christ.

2 Peter 1:11

Then the King will say to those on his right, Come, you who are blessed by my Father; take your inheritance, the kingdom prepared for you since the creation of the world.

Matthew 25:34

The Kingdom is Within

The German theologian Adolph Von Harnock who died in 1930 proposed that the Kingdom of God was limited to an inner spiritual dimension within those who were "born again". He denied the miracles of Jesus, rejected the Gospel of John and saw the outworking of the inner kingdom through a "Social Gospel". Scriptures that shaped this view are:

For the kingdom of God is not a matter of eating and drinking, but of righteousness, peace and joy in the Holy Spirit.

Romans 14: 17

This Scripture also supported Dodd's claim that the Kingdom is a present reality.

In reply Jesus declared, "I tell you the truth, no one can see the kingdom of God unless he is born again."

John 3:3

The Kingdom is the Church

A further view is based upon the theological position held by Augustine in the fourth century. He was one of the most influential theologians of church history and was the originator of the concept of original sin and free grace.

He considered the church to be the Kingdom of God and therefore as the church grew in number and influence so the Kingdom of God also increased and extended into the world.

The teachings of Augustine are in fact the seed bed of a number of current theological positions concerning the church, the Kingdom of God and the ways in which the church is to interface with the world at large. We shall develop the implications of this viewpoint later.

It would seem therefore that the Scriptures are used to support several different interpretations of the nature and the extent of the Kingdom of God. Rather than this be the cause of confusion, could it be an indication perhaps that the truth lies somewhere in an amalgamation of the various schools of thought?

Resolving the Issues

There seems to be little conflict in accepting the notion that whilst the Kingdom of God is indeed of an eternal nature, the experiential evidence may vary at different times and seasons.

It is possible to experience an entry into the Kingdom of God, through salvation, and yet not experience the "fullness" of what is yet to come.

It is also possible that the Kingdom of God is "at hand" and yet be commanded by the Lord Jesus to pray the Kingdom "come".

A clearer understanding can be reached by taking regard of what the Bible terms as "this age" and "the age to come."

5

The Ages

Although the Kingdom of God is the eternal rule and reign of God over all creation, the Bible clearly indicates that there are periods in which the expression of the Kingdom varies. These are referred to in the following scriptures as "ages".

> *Anyone who speaks a word against the Son of Man will be forgiven, but anyone who speaks against the Holy Spirit will not be forgiven, either in this age or in the age to come.*

> Matthew 12:32

> *"I tell you the truth," Jesus said to them, "no one who has left home or wife or brothers or parents or children for the sake of the kingdom of God will fail to receive many times as much in this age and, in the age to come, eternal life."*

> Luke 18:29-30

Jesus replied, "The people of this age marry and are given in marriage. But those who are considered worthy of taking part in that age and in the resurrection from the dead will neither marry nor be given in marriage."

Luke 20:34

We do, however, speak a message of wisdom among the mature, but not the wisdom of this age or of the rulers of this age, who are coming to nothing. No, we speak of God's secret wisdom, a wisdom that has been hidden and that God destined for our glory before time began. None of the rulers of this age understood it, for if they had, they would not have crucified the Lord of glory.

1 Corinthians 2:6-8

In fact the Apostle Paul even goes so far as to say that there is a "god" of "this age" who has power over the minds of unbelievers to the extent that they are blinded to the gospel.

The god of this age has blinded the minds of unbelievers, so that they cannot see the light of the gospel of the glory of Christ, who is the image of God.

2 Corinthians 4:4

The Problem of Mistranslation

The verses quoted above are from the New International Version and in each case they include the word "age". This varies from some other translations where they substitute "age" for "world". It is important that we understand and clarify the significance of the different translations.

The Ages

The error has occurred through using the word "world" as a direct translation of the Greek word *aion* which should more accurately be rendered "age" or "era". The significance of the word is relative to the spiritual or moral characteristics of the period of time rather than the actual length of time that is elapsed.

If the use of the word "world" were to be supported then the original text should contain the Greek word *kosmos*. The word *kosmos* denotes, not an "age" or an "era" but rather that which pertains to the earth in contrast to that which pertains to heaven.

The word "world" is a correct translation of *kosmos (or a derivative)* in the following verses. There are of course many other verses that translate *kosmos* as "world" but we shall limit ourselves to the following few in order to establish the importance of understanding the significant difference between "world" and "age". The importance of this difference will be explained in the next chapter.

> *In those days Caesar Augustus issued a decree that a census should be taken of the entire Roman world. (This was the first census that took place while Quirinius was governor of Syria.) And everyone went to his own town to register.*
>
> Luke 2:1-3

> *Again, the devil took him to a very high mountain and showed him all the kingdoms of the world and their splendour. "All this I will give you," he said, "if you will bow down and worship me."*
>
> Matthew 4:10

In these verses the reference is clearly to the world as the physical place where earthly kingdoms exist as opposed to a spiritual entity or indeed a period of existence.

The next verse to be considered contains a reference to the totality of this present world as something that can be gained as wealth. However it then warns of a time in the future, when the "Son of Man" (a reference to the glorified Jesus) will come into this physical world and establish His Kingdom.

> *What good will it be for a man if he gains the whole world, yet forfeits his soul? Or what can a man give in exchange for his soul? For the Son of Man is going to come in his Father's glory with his angels, and then he will reward each person according to what he has done. I tell you the truth, some who are standing here will not taste death before they see the Son of Man coming in his kingdom.*

> Matthew 16:26-28

There is a very interesting use of both *kosmos* and *aion* in this next verse to be considered.

> *He answered, "The one who sowed the good seed is the Son of Man. The field is the world (kosmos) and the good seed stands for the sons of the kingdom. The weeds are the sons of the evil one, and the enemy who sows them is the devil. The harvest is the end of the age,(aion) and the harvesters are angels.*

> Matthew 13:37-39

It can be established through the correct usage of the two words "age" and "world" that they do not refer to the same thing, but rather two distinct entities. The "world" being the summation of the physical creation and its spiritual condition, whilst "age" refers to the different "eras" in which the world experiences change. The Bible indicates that there are two "ages". It refers to "this age" and also to "the age to come". The main significance of the two ages is embodied in an understanding of the different levels of spiritual authority under which the world is governed.

This Age and the Age to Come

The verse which we have just considered in Matthew 13:39 contains a reference to the "end of the age". This implies that there will be an end of one age, or era, and the beginning of another. In fact, as we have already considered, this is clearly stated in Matthew 12:32.

> *Anyone who speaks a word against the Son of Man will be forgiven, but anyone who speaks against the Holy Spirit will not be forgiven, either in this age or in the age to come.*

> Matthew 12:32

A verse that reinforces the notion that there is a present age which will end and another age that will begin in the future is found in Ephesians 1:21.

> *...far above all rule and authority, power and dominion, and every title that can be given, not only in the present age but also in the one to come.*

> Ephesians 1:21

Understanding the context of this verse is important if we are to fully appreciate the implications of it relative to what the church is called to be in this "age". This understanding is essential if we are to fully appreciate the extent of God's parameters of spiritual authority within which the church can currently exercise dominion. This will be considered in more detail in later chapters when we examine how the Kingdom of God in this "age" relates to the cultures of this "world".

The context as presented by the Apostle Paul is his prayerful passion that the New Testament believers would become fully aware, not only of the glorious triumph of the risen Christ, but also the present position of Christ in 'this age' and also in the "age to come".

Furthermore he asserts that not only is Christ risen above all rule, authority, power and dominion in this age and the age to come, but that the risen Christ is also the Head of the Church, which is, notice the present tense, the fullness of Him who fills everything in every way.

These are such powerful truths that the Apostle Paul says he has not stopped praying that the believers at Ephesus would catch the revelation of what it means. Please read them slowly and ask the Holy Spirit to bring fresh revelation and understanding to you that will empower your life, your witness and your ministry.

If you are passionate about impacting the world around you with the power of the Kingdom of God then take this prayer of Paul and pray it over yourself. I often take these words and pray that I might know, understand and live out the reality of my calling as a disciple of Jesus. Let the Word of God and the Spirit of God empower you and release you for mighty exploits!

The Ages

For this reason, ever since I heard about your faith in the Lord Jesus and your love for all the saints, I have not stopped giving thanks for you, remembering you in my prayers. I keep asking that the God of our Lord Jesus Christ, the glorious Father, may give you the Spirit of wisdom and revelation, so that you may know him better.

I pray also that the eyes of your heart may be enlightened in order that you may know the hope to which he has called you, the riches of his glorious inheritance in the saints, and his incomparably great power for us who believe. That power is like the working of his mighty strength, which he exerted in Christ when he raised him from the dead and seated him at his right hand in the heavenly realms, far above all rule and authority, power and dominion, and every title that can be given, not only in the present age but also in the one to come. And God placed all things under his feet and appointed him to be head over everything for the church, which is his body, the fullness of him who fills everything in every way.

Ephesians 1:15-21

Praise God for the "incomparably" great power that was demonstrated over sin and death by the resurrection of Jesus from the tomb and His ascension to the place of all authority and power. Praise God again for the glorious reality that the church is also raised with Him to that place of authority, not as some future promise, but as a present reality in this age.

51

Kingdom and Culture

As the aim of this book is to explore the relationship of the Kingdom of God and the cultures of this world we shall return to these Scriptures and discover the extent, and the practical application of this awesome privilege and responsibility.

6

Proclamation
of the Kingdom

At the time of Jesus the Jews in Palestine were living under Roman occupation. The Scriptures (Old Testament) pointed them to hope for an overthrow of Roman rule and a restoration of a king from the line of Judah.

Many Jews saw the Messianic prophecies as promises to that end. The expectation of many would have been that the promised Messiah would enter as a victorious God appointed king to deliver them from their captivity. The hope was that He would come and establish a new political kingdom for them. In reality this still remains the case today for those who reject Jesus as the Messiah.

It was into this expectation that John the Baptist appeared with a message of imminent fulfillment.

> *In those days John the Baptist came, preaching in the Desert of Judea and saying, "Repent, for the kingdom of heaven is near." This is he who was spoken of through the prophet Isaiah: "A*

voice of one calling in the desert, `Prepare the way for the Lord, make straight paths for him.'"

Matthew 3:1

Not only did John proclaim the imminence of the Kingdom but he also identified Jesus as the one who would bring the promised fulfillment.

Finally they said, "Who are you? Give us an answer to take back to those who sent us. What do you say about yourself?" John replied in the words of Isaiah the prophet, "I am the voice of one calling in the desert, `Make straight the way for the Lord.' "

Now some Pharisees who had been sent questioned him, "Why then do you baptize if you are not the Christ, nor Elijah, nor the Prophet?"

"I baptize with water," John replied, "but among you stands one you do not know. He is the one who comes after me, the thongs of whose sandals I am not worthy to untie."

This all happened at Bethany on the other side of the Jordan, where John was baptizing.

The next day John saw Jesus coming toward him and said, "Look, the Lamb of God, who takes away the sin of the world! This is the one I meant when I said, `A man who comes after me has surpassed me because he was before me.' I myself did not know him, but the reason I came baptizing with water was that he might be revealed to Israel."

John 1:22-31

Proclamation of the Kingdom

It was this perceived threat to the Roman occupation of Israel that the Pharisees would use some three years later to accuse Jesus of treason against Caesar. They brought Him before Pilate for questioning and it was on this very point that He was accused of being a criminal.

> *Pilate then went back inside the palace, summoned Jesus and asked him, "Are you the king of the Jews?"*
>
> *"Is that your own idea," Jesus asked, "or did others talk to you about me?"*
>
> *"Am I a Jew?" Pilate replied. "It was your people and your chief priests who handed you over to me. What is it you have done?"*
>
> *Jesus said, "My kingdom is not of this world. If it were, my servants would fight to prevent my arrest by the Jews. But now my kingdom is from another place."*
>
> *"You are a king, then!" said Pilate.*
>
> *Jesus answered, "You are right in saying I am a king. In fact, for this reason I was born, and for this I came into the world, to testify to the truth. Everyone on the side of truth listens to me."*
>
> *"What is truth?" Pilate asked. With this he went out again to the Jews and said, "I find no basis for a charge against him. But it is your custom for me to release to you one prisoner at the time of the Passover. Do you want me to release `the king of the Jews'?"*

John 18:33-39

Throughout His ministry Jesus had taught in parables relating spiritual truths about the Kingdom in stories that the culture of his time could relate to. Some of His teaching remained a mystery however to those who were spiritually blind.

Here in this passage Jesus clearly explains that the Kingdom He has come to establish is not an earthly one, but rather one of another world. He was not on a mission to merely release Israel from Roman occupation. His mission was far more reaching than that. Jesus came to set the whole world free from the dominion of Satan and to establish a spiritual Kingdom on earth that would transcend all natural kingdoms.

Jesus Proclaimed the Kingdom

From the outset of His ministry Jesus made the Kingdom of God His priority not only in proclamation but also in demonstration.

From that time on Jesus began to preach, "Repent, for the kingdom of heaven is near."

Matthew 4:17

Jesus went throughout Galilee, teaching in their synagogues, preaching the good news of the kingdom, and healing every disease and sickness among the people. News about him spread all over Syria, and people brought to him all who were ill with various diseases, those suffering severe pain, the demon-possessed, those having seizures, and the paralyzed, and he healed them. Large crowds from Galilee, the Decapolis, Jerusalem, Judea and the region across the Jordan followed him.

Matthew 4:23-25

This was not Jesus telling people that in three year's time He would die and then they could go to heaven. This was not just telling them about a God in heaven who loved them. This was not just telling them they needed to be "born again."

This was a demonstration in the here and now (or to be more accurate in the there and then) of a different order coming into the world. This was a direct confrontation, a power encounter, between two opposing kingdoms. It was the direct challenge of God's authority against the authority of the "ruler of this present age". This was God declaring that the time had come for one "age" to pass and another "age" to come. This was God demonstrating His ultimate and absolute authority over all of His creation.

For a time God, in His permissive will, had permitted Satan to have a level of authority over creation as a consequence of Adam's sin. The principle of Kingdom authority will be covered in the next chapter.

In Jesus God had set His appointed time for the salvation of mankind and for the beginning of the end for the rule of Satan on the earth. This would be finally completed at the return of Christ in glory.

Jesus clearly saw that His mission was to confront the kingdom of Satan head on and to demonstrate the greater authority and power of the Kingdom of God.

> *But if I drive out demons by the finger of God,*
> *then the kingdom of God has come to you.*

> Luke 11:20

Kingdom and Culture

7

Authority
of the Kingdom

A dictionary definition of authority is rendered as *"the power to command, control, or judge others"*. If that is the case, then ultimate authority must rest with the God of all creation by whose command the earth was formed along with all that is contained therein. The psalmist understood this and made a very clear statement in Psalm 24.

> *The earth is the LORD's, and everything in it, the world, and all who live in it; for he founded it upon the seas and established it upon the waters.*
>
> Psalm 24:1-2

When writing to the believers at Colosse, the Apostle Paul wrote about Jesus in a way that describes not only the oneness of the Father and the Son but also the ultimate supremacy of the Godhead in all things.

> *For by him all things were created: things in heaven and on earth, visible and invisible,*

whether thrones or powers or rulers or authorities; all things were created by him and for him. He is before all things, and in him all things hold together. And he is the head of the body, the church; he is the beginning and the firstborn from among the dead, so that in everything he might have the supremacy.

Colossians 1:16-18

There is a particular Scripture in Matthew 8 that gives a very clear account of how the principle of authority works. In this passage we read of an encounter Jesus had with a Roman centurion. The centurion was a man of considerable importance in the Roman military and therefore one accustomed to the principles of authority. It is from this passage that we learn the vital lesson on the subject of authority.

When Jesus had entered Capernaum, a centurion came to him, asking for help. "Lord," he said, "my servant lies at home paralyzed and in terrible suffering." Jesus said to him, "I will go and heal him." The centurion replied, "Lord, I do not deserve to have you come under my roof. But just say the word, and my servant will be healed. For I myself am a man under authority, with soldiers under me. I tell this one, `Go,' and he goes; and that one, `Come,' and he comes. I say to my servant, `Do this,' and he does it." When Jesus heard this, he was astonished and said to those following him, "I tell you the truth, I have not found anyone in Israel with such great faith. I say to you that many will come from the east and the west, and will take their places at the feast with Abraham,

> *Isaac and Jacob in the kingdom of heaven. But the subjects of the kingdom will be thrown outside, into the darkness, where there will be weeping and gnashing of teeth." Then Jesus said to the centurion, "Go! It will be done just as you believed it would." And his servant was healed at that very hour.*
>
> Matthew 8:5-13

The lesson is clear. It is simply that in order to exercise authority "over" others, one must first be "under" authority oneself.

This centurion explained that he was first a man who was submitted to a higher authority from which he was granted the right to exercise authority over those under his own command. To grasp this simple, but profound lesson is to discover the key to effective spiritual warfare. This truth is clearly spelled out for us in the book of James.

> *Submit yourselves, then, to God. Resist the devil, and he will flee from you.*
>
> James 4:7

It is through submitting to God's sovereignty in our own lives that we are then able to exercise authority over Satan and his principalities and powers. The exercise of this authority in spiritual warfare will be considered in a later chapter under the heading "Invasion" as we consider how God's Kingdom impacts society and the effect that has upon our culture and the communities in which we live.

Jesus and Authority

As we look at the life of Jesus we see that He lived with His will totally surrendered to the will of the Father. This was the key to the great authority that He exercised over the spiritual, and in fact, over the natural world.

> *So Jesus said, "When you have lifted up the Son of Man, then you will know that I am the one I claim to be and that I do nothing on my own but speak just what the Father has taught me. [29] The one who sent me is with me; he has not left me alone, for I always do what pleases him."*

> John 8:28-29

In the Garden of Gethsemane we find this truth so passionately enacted. At the point of His imminent betrayal that was to lead Him to Calvary, Jesus chose to submit His will to the Father. This was no easy thing, but rather a decision that was wrought in the depths of anguish as His sweat turned to blood. What an example and an inspiration for us as we seek to honour the Father's will in all we do in our own lives.

> *Jesus went out as usual to the Mount of Olives, and his disciples followed him. On reaching the place, he said to them, "Pray that you will not fall into temptation." He withdrew about a stone's throw beyond them, knelt down and prayed, "Father, if you are willing, take this cup from me; yet not my will, but yours be done." An angel from heaven appeared to him and strengthened him. And being in anguish, he prayed more earnestly, and his sweat was like drops of blood falling to the ground.*

> Luke 22:39-44

It is at the times of greatest temptation that we can win the greatest victories. It is when we can say, like Jesus, *"Father, if you are willing, take this cup from me; yet not my will, but yours be done".*

Positional Authority

Positional authority is *"the power to command, control, or judge others"* by virtue of being the incumbent of an office that has been invested with such authority. It is the office to which others must submit rather than the individual who at any time may hold such office.

A simple illustration from my own personal experience is that of the rank structure within the military. At every level of promotion to a higher rank came an investiture of greater authority and the exercise of wider influence. This "positional authority" only exists however within the parameters of the rules or laws that govern the particular organisation.

The authority that Jesus exercised during His life and ministry on earth was not a "Positional Authority". It was not even as a result of His victory on the cross. This was an event yet to happen.

His "incarnation" was as a human being. The Bible tells us that He laid aside His majesty and lived on this earth with the temptations and challenges that we all face.[6] Throughout His life on earth it was as a man that His attitude and integrity were completely submitted to God. In this way He would be an example to all who would follow Him.

In writing to the Philippians the apostle Paul encourages the believers to have the same attitude as Christ with regard to

---

[6] This is known as the "Kenosis Theory"

submission to God's will in their lives. This submission of Jesus led ultimately to His exaltation above every other name.

> *Your attitude should be the same as that of Christ Jesus: Who, being in very nature God, did not consider equality with God something to be grasped, but made himself nothing, taking the very nature of a servant, being made in human likeness. And being found in appearance as a man, he humbled himself and became obedient to death – even death on a cross! Therefore God exalted him to the highest place and gave him the name that is above every name, that at the name of Jesus every knee should bow, in heaven and on earth and under the earth, and every tongue confess that Jesus Christ is Lord, to the glory of God the Father.*

> Philippians 2:5-11

As mature sons and daughters of the Living God we are called to exercise spiritual authority, but we can only do this as we submit our lives, our wills and our passions to the will of the Father.

The Disciples and Authority

Throughout the Gospels we read of the many multitudes that followed Jesus as He travelled around proclaiming the Kingdom of Heaven, driving out demons, feeding the hungry, healing the sick and even raising the dead. What an amazing journey it was to walk with Jesus then, and what an amazing journey it is to walk with Him today also.

However, it was not to the multitudes that He invested Kingdom authority, but to a much smaller number called His disciples. In much the same way that a "Rabbi" would gather his own group of followers, or adherents, Jesus gathered His twelve disciples to Himself.

The word "disciple" is one that denotes a "learner". It is someone who has committed themselves to a teacher, not only in a cerebral exercise but rather in a whole life commitment. It was in this manner that Jesus trained His small band of disciples in whom He would invest not only His message of the Kingdom, but also His mantle of authority.

Even before His victory over sin and death at Calvary which would ultimately release "positional authority" to His disciples, Jesus was able to invest the same authority to them that He Himself carried. This was an authority they gained through their commitment and submission to their master, Jesus, who was Himself in turn submitted to God.

Notice in the following verses that Jesus called His disciples "to Him" and then sent them out "from Him". It is only as disciples submit "to" the master that they can receive "from" Him.

> *He called his twelve disciples to him and gave*
> *them authority to drive out evil spirits and to*
> *heal every disease and sickness.*
>
> Matthew 10:1

A few verses later we read the instructions that He gave them. They were in fact called to do the very same works that Jesus had been performing up to this point.

> *As you go, preach this message: 'The kingdom*
> *of heaven is near.' Heal the sick, raise the dead,*
> *cleanse those who have leprosy, drive out*
> *demons. Freely you have received, freely give.*
>
> Matthew 10:7-8

This is exactly what happened as the disciples went out in the authority that had been granted then through their commitment and discipleship to Jesus. However powerful this investiture of authority was to the disciples, it was in fact just another step in their preparation as "learners" in the workings of the Kingdom. There would come another level when the full impact of their calling would be realized.

Ultimate Submission – Ultimate Authority

For Jesus Calvary was to be the final act of ultimate submission. In the Garden of Gethsemane Jesus had submitted to the will of the Father. He had been tortured emotionally as proven by the burst blood vessels that mingled with the sweat of His brow.

However traumatic that was for Him, it was but a foretaste of that which was to come. The prophet Isaiah some 600 years before had prophesied of the Messiah as a "suffering servant" willing to lay down His life in submission to the Master's plan.

> *He was despised and rejected by men, a man of sorrows, and familiar with suffering. Like one from whom men hide their faces he was despised, and we esteemed him not. Surely he took up our infirmities and carried our sorrows, yet we considered him stricken by God, smitten by him, and afflicted. But he was pierced for our transgressions, he was crushed for our iniquities; the punishment that brought us peace was upon him, and by his wounds we are healed. We all, like sheep, have gone astray, each of us has turned to his own way; and the*

Lord has laid on him the iniquity of us all. He was oppressed and afflicted, yet he did not open his mouth; he was led like a lamb to the slaughter, and as a sheep before her shearers is silent, so he did not open his mouth.

Isaiah 53:3-7

It was because of this act of ultimate submission that we can remind ourselves of the Apostle Paul's words in Philippians 2.

And being found in appearance as a man, he humbled himself and became obedient to death – even death on a cross! Therefore God exalted him to the highest place and gave him the name that is above every name, that at the name of Jesus every knee should bow, in heaven and on earth and under the earth, and every tongue confess that Jesus Christ is Lord, to the glory of God the Father.

Philippians 2:8-11

It was because of His total submission to the Father in all things that Satan was unable to have any hold over Jesus. At His incarnation Jesus voluntarily laid down the claims of His divinity, so that it was not as God that He walked in the flesh on this earth, but as a man. His power and authority was sourced in the fact that He was tempted in every way and yet "without sin". He was truly the only one ever to have lived who was qualified to pay the entirety of the total debt owed to the justice of God.

Because Jesus was without sin and yet humbled Himself as a ransom for it, He was able to satisfy the demands of God's judgment and therefore pay the full quota assigned to the death sentence handed down to mankind through Adam.

Having qualified for authority through submission in His lifetime, Jesus was now to be granted "all authority" through His resurrection from the dead.

His resurrection through every spiritual rank and principality was proof indeed that sin had no hold over Him whatsoever. The way was now open for a period of Kingdom rule on the earth through the principle of "Positional Authority".

8

Positional Authority
and the Kingdom

We have already formulated an understanding of positional authority. It is *"the power to command, control, or judge others"* by virtue of being the incumbent of an office that has been invested with such authority. It is the office to which others must submit rather than the individual who at any time may hold such office.

Scripture is very clear regarding the positional authority that Jesus attained through His resurrection. There are many passages in the New Testament that describe the position now held by the glorified, risen and ascended Lord Jesus. We have already read that *"God exalted him to the highest place and gave him the name that is above every name"*, but there are few verses however that ring with such glorious clarity as those found in Ephesians.

In describing the power of God at work towards believers the Apostle Paul likens it to the incomparably great power exercised by God in the resurrection of Jesus from the dead.

That power is like the working of his mighty strength, which he exerted in Christ when he raised him from the dead and seated him at his right hand in the heavenly realms, far above all rule and authority, power and dominion, and every title that can be given, not only in the present age but also in the one to come. And God placed all things under his feet and appointed him to be head over everything for the church, which is his body, the fullness of him who fills everything in every way.

Ephesians 1:19-23

From that moment Jesus was "positioned" above every other authority structure in the entirety of eternity. It is from that ultimate position of authority that He now presides as the head over everything in all creation and here the particular emphasis is that as head of the church. We shall consider the implications that this has for the church shortly, but for the present let us consider the immediate effect this had upon His disciples whom, in the immediate aftermath of His crucifixion, seemed to be uncertain as to their future.

Positional Authority and the Great Commission

Although Jesus had sent out His disciples to replicate His ministry during His lifetime, the time had now come for another dispensation of authority to commence.

After His ascension Jesus appeared to His disciples and gave them what has become known as "the Great Commission".

All authority in heaven and on earth has been given to me. Therefore go and make disciples of all nations, baptizing them in the name of the

70

*Father and of the Son and of the Holy Spirit,
and teaching them to obey everything I have
commanded you. And surely I am with you
always, to the very end of the age.*

Matthew 28:18-20

There are principally three sections to this Great Commission
of Jesus to His disciples. Firstly there is the mandate, then the
mission and thirdly there is the method. We shall revisit the
Great Commission in a later chapter when we consider how the
Kingdom is to impact culture. At that point we shall address
the mission and the method in some detail but sufficient for the
present to address the issues relating to authority, hence the
mandate.

Mandate

A dictionary definition of the word mandate reads as follows:
*"an official or authoritative command to carry out a particular
task".*
Clearly there is a task involved here, the making of disciples,
but our focus in this section is on the authority aspect of the
mandate.

The word *"all"* leaves little doubt as to the extent of the
authority that Jesus now carries. He is the absolute in all things.
The use of the term *"in heaven and on earth"* is also very
interesting in that it covers the spheres in which the disciples
were themselves to exercise the authority soon to be invested in
them.

The disciples were not only to represent their spiritual leader,
their "Rabbi", but now they were to represent the whole of
heaven itself. This surely is what Jesus meant when He gave

them the authority to baptize in the *"name of the Father and the Son and the Holy Spirit"*.

In The Name Of

Here Jesus gives the disciples the mandate to act on the authority of the "trinity", which is a term representing the absolute authority and follows the sense of the *"all's"* in this passage. Depending on the particular translations the word *"all"* is used to describe authority, nations, things, and days. The emphasis is to send the message that this is no little task, but one that will have eternal implications.

To act *"in the name of"* a person or an organization is to take on the responsibility of executing their will, their intentions, and their opinions, in any given situation. This is the ambassadorial role of a nation's embassy staff, or the responsibility of nominated executors for the estate of a deceased person. It is to act in the same way that the person would themselves act if they were confronted with the same situation. This is an implicit requirement in the granting of authority to the disciples who were to act on behalf of Jesus and the Kingdom.

The disciples therefore, were not only commissioned to go and "tell" people about Jesus and the Kingdom of Heaven, but they were to be the full representation of Jesus and of the Kingdom. The Book of Acts gives some examples of how the disciples fulfilled this commission.

How they carried out this mandate can be clearly seen from the very first encounter that Peter and John had to represent Jesus in this way. The account is found in Acts three.

> *One day Peter and John were going up to the temple at the time of prayer, at three in the*

afternoon. Now a man crippled from birth was being carried to the temple gate called Beautiful, where he was put every day to beg from those going into the temple court. When he saw Peter and John about to enter, he asked them for money. Peter looked straight at him, as did John. Then Peter said, "Look at us!" So the man gave them his attention, expecting to get something from them.

Then Peter said, "Silver or gold I do not have, but what I have I give you. In the name of Jesus Christ of Nazareth, walk." Taking him by the right hand, he helped him up, and instantly the man's feet and ankles became strong. He jumped to his feet and began to walk. Then he went with them into the temple courts, walking and jumping, and praising God. When all the people saw him walking and praising God, they recognized him as the same man who used to sit begging at the temple gate called Beautiful, and they were filled with wonder and amazement at what had happened to him.

Acts 3:1-10

In this passage we see that Peter and John were confronted with a physically disabled beggar who was accustomed to begging at the same place every day. In all probability the disciples had encountered this man before, but something had now changed.

On this occasion they did not limit themselves to the beggar's own requests but went beyond that into a higher level of provision. They would give to him, not out of the level of their own resources, but out of the resources of the Kingdom of

Heaven which they now represented. This Kingdom is not limited to human provision, but to God's unlimited provision.

The disciples' response is simple yet profound. They could not meet the man's needs from their own resources but they could change his life with the resources of the One Whom they now represented, whose name they were now empowered to use. What an amazing revelation Peter had at this point.

> *Then Peter said, "Silver or gold I do not have, but what I have I give you. In the name of Jesus Christ of Nazareth, walk."*

> Verse 6

When Peter used the term *"in the name of Jesus"* it was not some nominal prayer formula, but a faith proclamation backed up by the highest authority in heaven and on earth. As such, Peter was representing Jesus at that moment in that situation. He was representing the "seat" of authority in which Jesus was now seated in heavenly places.

The crowd that witnessed this miracle were amazed and astonished at what had happened. They questioned Peter and John as to how this healing had happened. Peter's response gives us the key.

> *By faith in the name of Jesus, this man whom you see and know was made strong. It is Jesus' name and the faith that comes through him that has given this complete healing to him, as you can all see.*

> Acts 3:16-17

This miracle, Peter explained, had been carried out *"in the name of Jesus"* as they had been His representatives at the beggar's point of need.

As ambassadors for Christ, the Christian church also carries this same mandate. The authority of the Great Commission was not restricted to just those early disciples but given to all who believe in Jesus. In the parallel passage in Mark we read these words of Jesus.

> *He said to them ,"Go into all the world and preach the good news to all creation. Whoever believes and is baptized will be saved, but whoever does not believe will be condemned. And these signs will accompany those who believe: In my name they will drive out demons; they will speak in new tongues; they will pick up snakes with their hands; and when they drink deadly poison, it will not hurt them at all; they will place their hands on sick people, and they will get well."*
>
> *Mark 16:15-18*

Here the specifics of what the disciples were to do is made somewhat clearer. They were not only to preach and proclaim truth but they were also to demonstrate the authority of the Kingdom over the spirit world and also over the "brokenness" of creation by healing sickness and disease.

In both accounts of the Great Commission we have a very clear mandate by Jesus to His followers to exercise Kingdom authority on His behalf in "all the world".

Positional Authority and the Church

A clear understanding of the positional authority of the New Testament church is absolutely vital if we are to see the Kingdom of God impact the world in these last days. It is fundamental to the strategic plan of God in these days that the church not only understands in "principle" but applies in "practice" the role that God has ordained for it.

At this point we shall consider the "principle" and then in part three we shall consider the "practice". The principle is very clear from Scripture, especially the following passages from the book of Ephesians.

It is that in just the same way as Christ has been exalted to the right hand of the Father, far above all rule, authority and power, the church has been raised up and seated with Him. It is from that co-location with Christ that we are to exercise spiritual authority as His representatives over the principalities and powers in the heavenly places.

> *I pray also that the eyes of your heart may be enlightened in order that you may know the hope to which he has called you, the riches of his glorious inheritance in the saints, and his incomparably great power for us who believe. That power is like the working of his mighty strength, which he exerted in Christ when he raised him from the dead and seated him at his right hand in the heavenly realms, far above all rule and authority, power and dominion, and every title that can be given, not only in the present age but also in the one to come. And God placed all things under his feet and appointed him to be head over everything for the church, which is his body, the fullness of him who fills everything in every way.*

Ephesians 1:18-23

In this passage there is a clear statement that Christ is in that place of ultimate authority at God's right hand. This is not of course a physical place but a description of positional authority. We then read that in that position, Jesus is also "head of the church", which is described as Christ's "body".

This is an interesting picture especially in the light of the phrase *"under his feet"*. We therefore have the "head" the "body" and then everything else under the "feet". This would suggest that the church is also in a position of authority above "all things". This statement might seem somewhat speculative until we read some more verses in Ephesians.

> *And God raised us up with Christ and seated us with him in the heavenly realms in Christ Jesus.*

> Ephesians 2:6

> *Although I am less than the least of all God's people, this grace was given me: to preach to the Gentiles the unsearchable riches of Christ, and to make plain to everyone the administration of this mystery, which for ages past was kept hidden in God, who created all things. His intent was that now, through the church, the manifold wisdom of God should be made known to the rulers and authorities in the heavenly realms, according to his eternal purpose which he accomplished in Christ Jesus our Lord.*

> Ephesians 3:8-11

Here we begin to see a picture emerging of the principle of church, not as an earthly organization, but as a heavenly "organism" filled with the vitality of the life of Christ, appointed and empowered with authority to represent Jesus the head, both on earth and also in the heavenly realms.

The "practice" of how this is achieved will be considered in part three when we consider how the church interacts both with the principalities and powers in the heavenly places and also with the different cultural influences within our modern day societies.

All the World

It is the church that is called to continue the Great Commission of Christ given to His first disciples. The commission has never been rescinded and indeed Jesus declared that He would be "with them", i.e. those fulfilling the Great Commission until the end of the age. The term "all the world" in the Great Commission is the link between the first and the second parts of this book.

Having considered some aspects of the Kingdom of God, we shall now begin to see how the Kingdom is to impact and to influence the world in which we live.

There is certainly much more to the Kingdom of God than has been discussed here but the aim has been to give enough background understanding to enable a clear appreciation of the role of the church in society, not just as a force for social change but as a powerful and authoritative representative of the Kingdom here on earth, today!

Part Two

Kingdom and Culture

9

Culture

The title of this book is *Kingdom and Culture*, and as such seeks to examine the extent to which the present experience of the Kingdom of God can influence and shape the world in which we live today.

The transforming power of God can be experienced at every level of our existence, both at an individual level and also at corporate and cultural levels, as the Holy Spirit leads believers to live as empowered representatives of the Kingdom of God on earth. The following chapters, I believe, outline God's Fivefold Strategy for change and transformation.

The strategy outlined has come together as I have journeyed along my own path of discovery, constantly seeking to be effective and relevant, whilst all the time listening to the heartbeat of the Father for His beloved creation.

It is a journey on which I have experienced the depths of frustration as I look out at a world, destroying itself as it submits to the ever destructive powers of the Kingdom of Darkness. The continual downward spiral of despair as the increase of lawlessness abounds with no apparent human means to arrest the weight of the tide.

Scripture describes this world as the domain of Satan. Within God's ultimate sovereignty, He has granted Satan a term of office through the rebellion of humanity since the fall of man. It is a world in which the values and ethics are influenced, not by the goodness of God but by the principles of sin. It is a world based on deception and human tradition rather than on the principles of the Kingdom of God. The following Scriptures give some insights.

> *For the wisdom of this world is foolishness in God's sight.*
>
> 1 Corinthians 3:19

> *I have written you in my letter not to associate with sexually immoral people – not at all meaning the people of this world who are immoral, or the greedy and swindlers, or idolaters. In that case you would have to leave this world.*
>
> 1 Corinthians 5:9-10

> *As for you, you were dead in your transgressions and sins, in which you used to live when you followed the ways of this world and of the ruler of the kingdom of the air, the spirit who is now at work in those who are disobedient. All of us also lived among them at one time, gratifying the cravings of our sinful nature and following its desires and thoughts. Like the rest, we were by nature objects of wrath.*
>
> Ephesians 2:1-3

Culture

See to it that no one takes you captive through hollow and deceptive philosophy, which depends on human tradition and the basic principles of this world rather than on Christ.

Colossians 2:8

In Galatians five the Apostle Paul very clearly describes the ways of this world and the moral values that it embraces.

I have also, on the other hand, along this journey, lived in the heights of abounding and overflowing joy as I have witnessed lives and situations, my own included, being radically transformed by the power of God in action.

As believers we need to be aware of the world around us. We are "in" the world but not "of" it. We are in that exciting interface of the two Kingdoms and it is here that we experience the amazing grace of God and the transforming power of the Word and of the Spirit.

Perhaps the clearest comparison of the two is found in Galatians chapter five where Paul is encouraging the believers not to live by the desires of the sinful nature but to be led in all things by the Holy Spirit.

So I say, live by the Spirit, and you will not gratify the desires of the sinful nature. For the sinful nature desires what is contrary to the Spirit, and the Spirit what is contrary to the sinful nature. They are in conflict with each other, so that you do not do what you want. But if you are led by the Spirit, you are not under law. The acts of the sinful nature are obvious: sexual immorality, impurity and debauchery; idolatry and witchcraft; hatred, discord, jealousy, fits of rage, selfish ambition, dissensions, factions and envy; drunkenness, orgies, and the like. I warn you, as I did before, that those who live like this will not inherit the kingdom of God.

But the fruit of the Spirit is love, joy, peace, patience, kindness, goodness, faithfulness, gentleness and self-control. Against such things there is no law. Those who belong to Christ Jesus have crucified the sinful nature with its passions and desires. Since we live by the Spirit, let us keep in step with the Spirit.

Galatians 5:16-21

It would come as no surprise to anyone except the most spiritually blind, that the condition and values of the world today do not reflect the benefits of the "goodness" declared by God at creation. The question then arises, can this trend be changed, and if so what is the role of the church as God's Kingdom representatives, God's ambassadors in this foreign land?

To answer that question we must first understand how society and culture is shaped today and then address the role of the Kingdom with respect to culture. Having considered some aspects of the Kingdom of God we shall now consider Culture. In Part Three we shall unfold God's exciting strategic plan and consider the central role the New Testament church has been commissioned to play.

Culture Examined

The term "culture" describes the ideas, customs, values and arts of any given society. In other words it is the culture that shapes the way any society operates. It is the culture that identifies the ethnicity of any particular people group.

The past fifty years has seen a significant rise in multi-culturalism within the developed world. This has been due to many factors such as the accessibility of intercontinental travel, commercial inter-dependence, and the desire of many nations to eradicate racism and promote social harmony. The opening of national borders within Europe and the influx of migrant workers to many nations has created a diverse mix of ethnic groupings within any one nation state.

This phenomenon is very interesting in the context of the Great Commission. Let us remind ourselves of the ongoing responsibility of the church.

> *Then Jesus came to them and said, "All authority in heaven and on earth has been given to me. Therefore go and make disciples of all nations, baptizing them in the name of the Father and of the Son and of the Holy Spirit, and teaching them to obey everything I have commanded you. And surely I am with you always, to the very end of the age."*

> Matthew 28:18-20

Our interest in this section of the book is to understand what Jesus was saying when He used the word "nations". Earlier in Matthew Jesus had sent out His twelve disciples on a limited mission to the lost sheep of Israel.

> *These twelve Jesus sent out with the following instructions: "Do not go among the Gentiles or enter any town of the Samaritans. Go rather to the lost sheep of Israel. As you go, preach this message: 'The kingdom of heaven is near.' Heal*

the sick, raise the dead, cleanse those who have leprosy, drive out demons. Freely you have received, freely give."

Matthew 10:5-8

Now at the end of His earthly ministry (chapter 28) Jesus extends the commission to "all nations". Here in Matthew 28 the original Greek language uses the word *"ethnos"* as opposed to the similar passage in Mark 16 which uses the word *"kosmos"*.

In Mark 16 the mandate is to go into all the "physical" world which has a more geographic implication, but here in Matthew 28 the word *"ethnos"* suggests that the commission of Jesus was for His disciples to go into all the different identifiable "people groups".

Historically, the mission field has been seen to be anywhere "overseas", somewhere in another geographical location. Countless thousands of Christians throughout the centuries have travelled all over the world to share the good news of Jesus Christ. A great number of these honourable servants of the Lord have paid with their own lives in their endeavours to reach the unreached, and they should forever be remembered with honour.

Today, with the rise of multi-culturalism we find that there is a vast array of "people groups" living within the same geographical location. The call to travel overseas and reach the geographical *"kosmos"* remains a valid ministry, but for many people, there is indeed a mission field much closer to home.

In fact the word *"ethnos"* is not limited to people groups of an identifiable nationality, but can apply to any group of people that gathers together with the same values, aspirations, goals, ideas, and customs.

Local Community "ethnos" Groups

Within any local community there will be a vast array of separate identifiable groupings that meet around a specific set of values, aspirations, principles etc that are unique to that group. Even a cursory glance at the local information bureau, or the local "what's on" type of information sheet will indicate the wide variety of separate groupings. Could it be that in commissioning the church into the *"ethnos"*, it has a calling to engage with the local community at this grass roots level as well as reaching the far flung corners of the geographical world?

In truth, the mission field is wherever we are and with whatever is "at hand". This is where the church should be engaged as "salt and light". As "salt" the church is to bring preservation and savour to the local community and as "light" to bring the revelation and the hope of God's love through Jesus Christ.

> *"You are the salt of the earth. But if the salt loses its saltiness, how can it be made salty again? It is no longer good for anything, except to be thrown out and trampled by men.*
>
> *"You are the light of the world. A city on a hill cannot be hidden. Neither do people light a lamp and put it under a bowl. Instead they put it on its stand, and it gives light to everyone in the house. In the same way, let your light shine before men, that they may see your good deeds and praise your Father in heaven.*
>
> Matthew 5:13-16

How the church is to achieve this Kingdom influence within the local community will be explained in Part Three when we look at God's Fivefold Strategic Plan.

10

The Seven Mountains

People fascinate me. I can spend hours at airports and other places where people from all over the world come together and congregate for a short time, but alas, never really meet.

What a vast array of nationalities and cultures, their uniqueness displayed sometimes by the colour of their skin, sometimes by their mode of dress, sometimes by their language and sometimes by the way they behave and carry their own individual identity and dignity.

I find it so interesting to examine the changes in my own reactions to the rich diversity of the different nationalities. In my early years I was brought up in a very loving and caring home, but sadly, with the benefit of hindsight, one that held some prejudiced opinions of other colours and cultures. Although I would not suggest my family were actively "racist", I would admit rather that we were "opinionated" through ignorance.

Over the years, certainly since my commitment to Jesus in 1978, I have come to see people of other cultures differently. I thank God that He has touched my own heart with His amazing grace and great love in such a way that I can truly say that I now see the world through different coloured lenses.

The one thing that unites us all beyond the sum total of our differences is that no matter our race, our colour or our creed every single individual is created by God, known by God and loved by God with a passion that sent Jesus to Calvary. If God *"so loved the world"* we too should aspire to do the same. The Great Commission may be God's mandate for the church, but it is as we gain His "compassion" that we find a motive that will move us to action.

> *Jesus went through all the towns and villages, teaching in their synagogues, preaching the good news of the kingdom and healing every disease and sickness. When he saw the crowds, he had compassion on them, because they were harassed and helpless, like sheep without a shepherd. Then he said to his disciples, "The harvest is plentiful but the workers are few. Ask the Lord of the harvest, therefore, to send out workers into his harvest field."*

> Matthew 9:35-38

The Great Commission should not be seen simply as a job to be done, but rather as a people to be reached. In order to effectively reach these different *"ethnos"* groups it is imperative that we understand what shapes them, their culture, their values, their language and their aspirations.

First Encounter with the Seven Mountains

It was sometime in 2009 that I was first introduced to the teaching relating to "The Seven Mountains". I picked up a book at a conference bookstall by Johnny Enlow in which he develops the concept first espoused by Bill Bright of Campus Crusade for Christ and Laurence Cunningham of YWAM some years earlier.[7]

Shortly after that I heard Che Ahn speak on the subject at a conference in England and then in January 2010 I attended the Pastors and Leaders conference at Toronto Airport Christian Fellowship where Dr Peter Wagner also spoke with great wisdom on the subject.

I have since also heard Lance Wallnau speak with great passion and clarity, bringing both biblical and prophetic insight accompanied by sound practical applications. I would strongly recommend the material produced by Lance Wallnau on this subject.

To all of these great ministries I am most grateful. The Lord has used them to bring to my attention what has been available, but alas, what has been hidden from my personal focus.

The reason I was so immediately drawn to the concept of the Seven Mountains is that at the close of my first book entitled *Adoption and Destiny*[8], I suggested that a "Mighty Church" need not be a "Mega Church" in respect of numbers, but rather one that represents the Kingdom of God in all the varied structures and activities of our societies and communities.

It seemed that the teaching regarding the Seven Mountains brought my passion for the church into some clear and workable strategy.

As I researched the available material and prayed for the Holy Spirit to bring revelation on the subject I began to become

---

[7] *The Seven Mountain Prophecy* by Johnny Enlow ISBN 978-1-59979-287-3
[8] *Adoption and Destiny* by Geoff Blease ISBN 978-190792-905-2
Previously published as the First edition entitled *Adoption, Sonship and The Family Business* in 2009

aware of some of the dangers and pitfalls that could possibly develop if I were to run ahead with unbridled enthusiasm without the constraint of a sound perspective with regard to the theology of the Kingdom of God.

The Seven Mountains Explained

The basis upon which the Seven Mountain teaching has developed is simply the acknowledgment that in any given culture there are principally seven main areas of influence that shape the values and development of that culture.

These are the "building blocks" or "shapers" of society and determine the values at the heart of communities and nations. As with people, the values at the heart of any community or nation will determine the actions of that people group. The wisdom of Proverbs supports this proposition.

> *Above all else, guard your heart, for it is the wellspring of life.*
>
> Proverbs 4:23

Put simply, it means that our core values will determine our behaviour.

The following diagram illustrates the "seven" principle areas of influence that shape the culture and societies in which we live, be it nations, local communities or even families. There are of course other things that have an influence but these are the seven principle factors that shape the way we live. Remember that *"ethnos"* means any identifiable people group that gathers to common values, visions and aspirations.

DIAGRAM 1 – The Seven Mountains

Explanation of Diagram 1

In diagram 1 the seven areas of influence are represented by the seven triangles which we shall refer to as the seven mountains. This diagram forms the basis of the teaching and will be built upon as a visual representation of God's Fivefold Strategy for the Kingdom of God to come and impact the world in which we live. A brief explanation of each of these mountains will be helpful at this stage.

11

The Mountain of Religion

Religion is defined as "the belief in or worship of, a supernatural power or powers considered to be divine or to have control over human destiny".[9]

From that definition it is evident that "religion" has been perhaps the strongest of all the influences that have shaped society and cultures down through the ages.

From the most primitive cave dwellers to the most sophisticated societies, religion has played a major part in shaping the values and principles by which that society functions.

Religion is a cultural system that creates powerful and long-lasting meaning at the very core of social groupings. Most religions will have narratives, symbols, traditions and sacred histories that give meaning to life or set out to explain the origin of life or the universe. It is from their perceived origins that they derive their principles of morality, ethics, religious laws and lifestyle practices. Although many religions call

---

[9] Collins *New English Dictionary*

adherents to a personal faith and commitment to the "higher power", there is also a strong public or community aspect to be considered.

Studies of history and archaeology would suggest that the development of ancient civilizations was strongly influenced by their centres of worship. As the people gathered to the places of worship other practical and social developments would take place to accommodate the needs of the people. In this way religion has been associated with the development of such public institutions as education, hospitals, the family, government, and political hierarchies.

In addition to the practical and social aspect of human development, religion has also influenced the more "cultural" aspirations of mankind. It is very clear to see that ever since the early artistic enterprise of the cave dwellers, religion has played a major part in influencing the ways in which humanity expresses outwardly, the deep inner passions of the soul. Perhaps the greatest expression of the way in which religion has influenced art can be seen in the incredible paintings of Michael Angelo in the Sistine Chapel in Rome.

Today, in many nations, religion and state are inseparable. The rise of Islam and the aspiration of that religion to impose Sharia Law is often perceived as a threat to other non Islamic states. Even within Islamic nations the different expressions of Islam is the cause of much civil unrest and human tragedy.

The nation of Israel continues to fight for its very existence based upon the Old Testament promises of geography and unfulfilled prophetic promises regarding the Messiah. These promises make Jerusalem the epicentre of their religious practices, the integrity of which is vital to Judaism.

The history of Christianity illustrates how the Great Commission of Jesus Christ to His disciples caused, not only the Christian faith to be found in the four corners of the world, but also much of the cultural and societal practices of the western civilizations.

The practices of Eastern Mysticism rose to world prominence in the 1960s, mainly through the influence of the Beatles pop group at that time. The austerity and hard times of the post war recovery period presented a golden opportunity for the "Fab Four" to exercise global influence. In fact in March 1966 John Lennon declared in an interview with Maureen Cleave from the *London Evening Standard* that the Beatles were "more popular then Jesus Christ."

The Beatles created such a cult following that wherever they led, millions of young people followed. Their exploits into Eastern Mysticism opened many religious and pseudo spiritual activities that deeply influenced the behaviour of not only their own generation, but many that were to follow.

We can conclude therefore from these brief considerations of the different religions, that it is appropriate to include religion in the list of "mountains" that influence the way cultures and societies are shaped and developed. However before we move on to explore the other "mountains" it would be appropriate to consider, under the heading of religion, both atheism and secularism.

Atheism

Although atheism is not by definition a "religion" because it claims there is no deity, we shall include it in our consideration of the mountain of religion on the grounds of association.

Although the term "atheism" originated in the ancient Greek in the form of "atheos" meaning "without god", it was first identified with a particular movement of the so called "free thinking" in the 18th century.

It is interesting to note that although the conceptions of atheism vary, some estimates agree that around 2.5% of the world's population would describe themselves as atheists. Although the accuracy of such estimates cannot be vouched for, the rates of self-reported atheism are among the highest in Western nations. European rates are estimated around Italy (7%), Spain (11%), Great Britain (17%), Germany (20%), and France (32%).

These figures would tend to endorse the notion that religion influences the way a society behaves. In Europe one of the leading nations in promoting secularism is France, the country that also embraces the highest level of atheism among its population.

Secularism

Secularism is the practice of separating the government of a nation state from the influences of religion. It claims to champion the freedom of the individual to choose their own destiny separate from religious influences or group expectations.

It aspires to free the individual from the dogma and bondage imposed by many religions and seeks to set the person free to choose from their own conscience. In its purest sense this is indeed something to be applauded, and is in fact, in many ways, commensurate with the teachings of Christianity as to the accountability of the individual person.

However, the purity of secularism has been difficult to maintain and it has in many cases become associated with the anti-religion aspirations of fundamentalist atheism.

Atheistic Secularism

Whilst "secularism" in its purest form has a positive aspiration for the rights of the individual, it appears to have become the province of the very negative intent of fundamentalist atheism to destroy the credibility of religion in society.

Atheistic Secularism is that dubious movement that whilst it champions the freedom for the individual, it in fact seeks to impose its own "anti God" agenda with the intent to shape society towards its own ends.

Kingdom and Culture

12

The Mountain of Government

In the social sciences, the term government refers to the particular group of people, the administrative bureaucracy, who control a (nation-)state at a given time, and the manner in which their governing organizations are structured.[10] We can also state that, governments are the means through which state power is employed.[11]

Clearly the "Mountain of Government" is hugely influential in shaping the way in which society develops. It not only directs policies according to the ideologies of the present incumbents but also has the power to embody those values and principles in the legal statutes of that nation state.

Historically the government of the United Kingdom, along with many other western nations, has been based upon the principles of Christianity. Many of the laws embodied in the

---

[10] Oxford English Dictionary (Online edition) Oxford University Press Nov 2010

[11] Flint, Colin & Taylor, Peter (2007). *Political Geography: World Economy, Nation-State, and Locality* (5th ed.). Pearson/Prentice Hall. p. 137. ISBN 978-0-13-196012-1.

constitution are rooted in Biblical values and aspire to create the basis of morality and the well-being of all citizens.

However, we can chart a progression of liberalism that has increasingly influenced the policies and the law making of successive governments. This liberalism in government has been a direct reflection on the attitudes of those individuals in government and the pressure of increasingly anti-Christian lobby groups.

These lobby groups represent all shades of interests, many of which are neutral with regard to Christian values. There are, however, also those lobby groups that seek to influence the government of the day that are far removed from the historical roots of Christian influence and against the accepted ethics of the "silent majority".

It is therefore vital for the Christian church to raise up key leaders who will aspire to enter into the corridors of power and be the people of influence who shape the values upon which the laws and government policies are made. We shall explore how this can be achieved when we consider God's Fivefold Strategy.

13

The Mountain of Education

The mountain of education is indeed a big one. The educational systems of most nations, whether primitive or advanced, will embrace the young people of that nation and influence their minds, values and attitudes that will be reflected in their lives as adults.

The word "educate" is rooted in the Latin "educare" which means to "lead forth; bring up; rear; train". By definition, education is any act or experience that has a formative effect on the mind, character or physical ability of an individual. Through education a society seeks to transmit its accumulated knowledge, its skills and values from one generation to another.

Clearly education is much more than mere knowledge regarding the accumulation of fact. Education also engages influence of the ethical values of a young person and upon their psychological and sociological development. The question to be asked by any parent, or indeed concerned citizen, is "who is shaping our children; how, and with what?"

The increasing popularity of faith schools across the religious spectrum seems to be an interesting commentary on the current education systems available in the nations. Could it be the reaction of many concerned parents who desire their children, not only to be informed as to "fact", but also to be trained and "led forth" within the values, ethics and practices espoused by a particular faith?

The probability is perhaps, that rather than a positive decision to acquire a faith based education, the concerned parent is seeking to protect and safeguard their child from the negative influences found in much of our secular educational establishments. This is not a criticism of the many excellent "educators" who work selflessly in our schools, but rather a comment on what many Christians perceive as the systemic liberal and atheistic precepts by which much of our educational curriculum is shaped.

The danger, however, as far as the Kingdom of God is concerned, is that instead of "reaching out" and shaping the wider education system, Christian educators are tempted to cluster into safe but narrow expressions of their expertise.

In unfolding God's Fivefold Strategy we shall discover how dedicated Christian educators can not only fulfil their educational expertise, but also extend Kingdom influence that can transform the way our education systems work.

14

The Mountain of Media

The term "Media" is used in the common usage sense of the "mass media" including radio, TV, films, the press, the internet and any other means by which news and information is communicated to the public.

We live in unsurpassed levels of access to information through all these different channels. The technology available today to an individual in the palm of their hand is almost limitless.

The internet and satellite TV communicate to the four corners of the earth unhindered by geophysical boundaries or political borders. These are unprecedented times, shrinking the global village even smaller almost daily.

The media, along with its comprehensive ability to inform, has an immense power to influence. Governments and newspaper tycoons have either aligned to propagate government policies, or opposed to discredit them. Similar party spirit is seen in the world of television and broadcasting in general.

As well as reporting and reflecting on politics the media carries great weight in shaping the social trends of people groups. Magazines abound with celebrity gossip and airbrushed pictures of how "Miss Perfect" should look, what size she should be and what she should be wearing. The media must take its share of responsibility for the tragic rise in the aspirations of many young impressionable people to live "pseudo" lives as they seek to be accepted by the false values of their peers.

The rise in Christian media is to be applauded, although not all of it is a true representation of the Kingdom of God. The endeavour to engage with the world in a contemporary way through modern technology can only be a positive step forward.

In fact as long ago as 1452 AD Christians were at the cutting edge of technology in their desire to communicate the Bible to the greater public. The first printing press was set up by Gutenberg in Mainz, Germany about the year 1452 AD and the first book to be printed on this printing press of the world was the Bible. Since that time the Bible has been the best-selling book in the world and continues to be so today.

As Christians in education have set up their own faith schools, so too Christians in the media should be applauded for the great influence they extend. However, the challenge today is not only to be "separate" from the world systems but to be "in" them. By being "in" but not "of" Christians can exert powerful influence on the world systems. Again we shall examine the possibilities when we unfold God's Fivefold Strategy.

It is very interesting to note that it has recently been announced by the University of Salford that they are to run a unique postgraduate course looking at how people engage and interact with the media and internet. The world is getting strategic about these things and the plea to the Christian church is not to hibernate in modern day "monasteries" but to engage with the process.

15

The Mountain of Arts and Entertainment

We have already seen how the pop phenomena of the Beatles in the 1960s changed forever the music scene and increased dramatically the impact that the pop culture has upon the young people of the world. Today, possibly more than ever, music is the catalyst that creates sub cultures and coalesces people from otherwise unconnected lifestyles into one cult following.

Soccer is also a huge influence across the globe and influences enormously the way people spend their time and their money. In some cases soccer teams are identified with specific religious or political allegiance, in which they become a very powerful influence.

Arts and Entertainment thrives on the "celebrity culture" which in turn reflects the huge sense of unfulfillment and dissatisfaction in the lives of those who follow so closely the lives of so called celebrities.

The rise in TV soap dramas and Reality TV creates environments of great social impact, albeit in many cases disconnected from 'reality' it seeks to portray. For many it can

107

be a source of vicarious satisfaction and success apart from the reality of their own lives. Life styles depicted on the screen are powerful tools of social influence and aspirations, but herein lies the danger.

Instead of retreating from these bastions of worldliness, Christian entertainers and entertainment experts should seek to engage with, and influence them at their very core.

16

The Mountain of Commerce

In the purest sense commerce is the buying and selling of goods, but we will extend that definition to a more general usage to include the wider activities engaged in the generation of wealth. It is this generation of wealth within a nation state that will ultimately pay for, and make viable, all of the other cultural influences of that nation.

It is indeed a truism that the one who holds the purse strings wields the power. It is, therefore, vital that "commerce" should not be the sole province of unregenerate entrepreneurs whose sole aim is to create personal wealth at the expense of the national well-being.

Recent events in the banking industry are a cause for great concern with regard to the vulnerability of the common good to the avarice of a few. There is indeed a pressing need for Kingdom values and Christian ethics to begin to influence the mountain of commerce.

For this to happen the Christians within the business world, the banking world and the other financial institutions will need to be equipped and prayerfully supported so that they can "lead for change".

This will mean much more than simply a "Christian presence" but rather the raising up of key people of influence in areas of commercial expertise who can make wise and ethical decisions whilst at the same time excelling in their given activity.

Lance Wallnau has a phrase *"proximity is power"*. How right he is. Another way of expressing the same sentiment would be *"you have to be in it to win it!"* Surely this is what Jesus meant when He called His disciples the *"salt of the earth"*. Salt that remains within the confines of a container serves no purpose until it is sprinkled.

For too long the church has been locked up in highly decorative salt cellars that get polished every Sunday morning. It is time for the salt to be sprinkled, not only in the Mountain of Commerce, but in all the seven Mountains of Influence.

17

The Mountain of Family

The final Mountain of Influence that we shall consider is that of the Family. We have kept this to the last, not because it is the least important, but because it is perhaps the most important.

It is into a family that a newborn baby is delivered at which time it is so incredibly vulnerable. The sense of well-being and nurture that is afforded to that young life in the early years will determine the morality, the ethics, the values and the aspirations of that child. This nurture will not only influence the child but will shape the adult that child will become.

What a tragedy then, to see the ever increasing degradation of family life in our societies today. It is not only the exponential increase in the number of unmarried mothers and single parents, neither is it the breakdown of communication between the generations within otherwise well-ordered families. It is not only the challenge of joblessness and unemployment, or absent fathers. It is not only the increasing isolationism and separation as each family member lives out their expression of family with an online "community" comprised of people they have never met in real life.

Family gives us our sense of belonging, our identity, our nurture, our security and comfort. It is when these are absent in the home that we become vulnerable in our search to satisfy these basic needs.

The Bible reflects God's heart for families. Throughout the scriptures there is a continual reference to families and genealogy. In the Book of Numbers the first chapter relates the account of the numbering of the nation of Israel two years into their wilderness wanderings. On each occasion a clan was numbered it refers to "families".

In Psalm 68 we find that God is described as a "father" and that He sees the family as the place of succor and security for the isolated and the lonely.

> *A father to the fatherless, a defender of widows,*
> *is God in his holy dwelling.*
>
> *God sets the lonely in families, he leads forth*
> *the prisoners with singing; but the rebellious*
> *live in a sun-scorched land.*
>
> Psalm 68:5-6

In many modern societies the traditional sense of family bears little resemblance to what happens in most homes. One of the main pressures on many households is financial. In order to meet the household budget both parents are forced to seek paid employment. This in turn means that young children are delivered to child minders early in the morning and received back by an exhausted parent just in time for a bath and bed and although they may be dearly loved by the parents, they receive limited parental nurture and sense of family.

Another consequence of the way we live today is that the different generations within the family are scattered geographically. The rise in mobility nationally and internationally has opened up world-wide opportunities on the one hand but a consequence is that the benefits of intergenerational relationships within families has been denied to many.

The rise in "care homes" and "residential homes for the elderly" is also an indication, rather than a cause, of the disintegration of the family in our modern societies.

These observations are made, not so much to rally support for a "back to basics" campaign, but rather to make the point that the family is a powerful influence on the way our societies are shaped and ordered. It is therefore vital that the Church should seek to not only "model" God's plan for the family, but also help others find restoration in this area.

Part Three

Kingdom and Culture

18

The Mountain of the Lord

In the last days the mountain of the Lord's temple will be established as chief among the mountains; it will be raised above the hills, and all nations will stream to it.

Isaiah 2:2

What is a "last days" prophecy to the nation of Israel doing heading up the chapter that begins to unfold God's Fivefold Strategy for the church? There is indeed good reason for this and it is hoped that the reader will catch something of God's heart not only for Israel in the "last days" but also for the church in these "present days".

Replacement theology strips the nation of Israel bare of the Old Testament prophetic promises of God and spiritualises them to a degree that is claimed can only be applied to the New Testament church.

The position taken here as we unfold God's Fivefold Strategy is, that whilst some prophecies can only be fulfilled through the nation of Israel, each one reveals God's heart and identifies spiritual principles that can be built upon by the New Testament church.

The prophecy from Isaiah 2:2 speaks of God's people being raised up to a position of leadership and influence within the world systems that will cause them to serve and to prosper the other nations.

This sense of leading and example is again restated much later by the same prophet.

> *Arise, shine, for your light has come, and the glory of the LORD rises upon you. See, darkness covers the earth and thick darkness is over the peoples, but the LORD rises upon you, and his glory appears over you. Nations will come to your light, and kings to the brightness of your dawn.*
>
> Isaiah 60:1-3

In a world of spiritual darkness, the people of God are called to arise and to shine, not to display their own prowess, but to radiate the glory of God with which they have been blessed.

God's presence cannot be separated from His glory, nor indeed from His power. Wherever God chooses to presence Himself, there His glory will be seen.

How wonderful it is then, for disciples of Jesus Christ to be blessed, not only with an external glory by association, but to be the very carriers of the Divine presence and the Divine glory.

Jesus told His disciples that the Holy Spirit would not only be "with them" and "upon them" but that the Holy Spirit would indeed be "flowing out from them" like a mighty rushing river.

> *On the last and greatest day of the Feast, Jesus stood and said in a loud voice, "If anyone is thirsty, let him come to me and drink. Whoever believes in me, as the Scripture has said,*

streams of living water will flow from within him." By this he meant the Spirit, whom those who believed in him were later to receive. Up to that time the Spirit had not been given, since Jesus had not yet been glorified.

John 7:37-39

The analogy of the Holy Spirit as a "river of living water" flowing from within the believer can be compared to the amazing passage in Ezekiel 47 where the benefits of that great river are described as healing and life giving. The whole passage warrants study but we will limit ourselves to the benefits released by this river starting at verse 7.

When I arrived there, I saw a great number of trees on each side of the river. He said to me, "This water flows toward the eastern region and goes down into the Arabah, where it enters the Sea. When it empties into the Sea, the water there becomes fresh. Swarms of living creatures will live wherever the river flows. There will be large numbers of fish, because this water flows there and makes the salt water fresh; so where the river flows everything will live.

Fishermen will stand along the shore; from En Gedi to En Eglaim there will be places for spreading nets. The fish will be of many kinds – like the fish of the Great Sea. But the swamps and marshes will not become fresh; they will be left for salt. Fruit trees of all kinds will grow on both banks of the river. Their leaves will not wither, nor will their fruit fail. Every month they will bear, because the water from the sanctuary flows to them. Their fruit will serve for food and their leaves for healing."

Ezekiel 47:7-12

To make the connection between John 7 and Ezekiel 47 is simply to show some of the practical benefits to those who come into close proximity to the Holy Spirit flowing out through the life of spirit filled Christians. No wonder Jesus declared His followers to be "lights of the world".

"You are the light of the world. A city on a hill cannot be hidden. Neither do people light a lamp and put it under a bowl. Instead they put it on its stand, and it gives light to everyone in the house. In the same way, let your light shine before men, that they may see your good deeds and praise your Father in heaven.

Matthew 5:14-16

It was never the intention of Jesus to gather groups of people together into Christian clusters simply to worship Him and grow spiritually "fat" with ever increasing knowledge of the Bible. It was His intention however, to call people from the pervading spiritual darkness of the world and make them into radiant beams of light shining as glorious examples of His grace and of His mercy.

It is only as the church "arises and shines" in the real world, that the Kingdom of God will impact the Seven Mountains of Culture. This is not only preaching a gospel of salvation, however vital that might be, and it certainly is, but becoming connected and involved with the world in which we live, giving wisdom, insight and guidance in a whole host of areas but especially in the Seven Mountains that shape the way we live. In this way the spiritual "principle" of the Mountain of the Lord will be established among the "nations".

19

God's Fivefold Strategy

In the previous chapters of this book I have attempted to give enough information regarding the Kingdom of God, Culture and the concept of the Seven Mountains, sufficient only to assist us in catching the simple principles of what I am now calling "God's Fivefold Strategy".

I have wrestled with the title of this section, i.e. "God's Fivefold Strategy" for fear of seeming to be presumptuous. However I do believe that the Holy Spirit has given me a degree of clarity on this subject and I submit to His Lordship and welcome His amazing grace!

I call it "God's" strategy simply because I find the five principles very clearly contained within scripture. It is as the Holy Spirit has led me over the years, that I have been able to piece together the various strands, although widely taught on an individual basis, and bring them together in an interlocking and co-ordinated strategy that can be clearly understood and practiced.

This strategy is not so that we can say we "have it" but rather that we can "do it". It is a practical step by step guide to becoming effective in releasing the Kingdom of God among the kingdoms of this world. It is not a theory, but has been born out in practice, and will give the reader a greater understanding of how to not only engage with God in intercession, but to also invade the principalities and powers in the heavenly realms before releasing Kingdom influence into the cultures in which we live.

In order to assist clarity of thought we shall consider each of the five sections in turn, each section beginning with the letter I. (Please forgive the preacher's alliteration at this point!)

We shall cover the sections in the following order:

- Identity
- Intimacy
- Intercession
- Invasion
- Influence

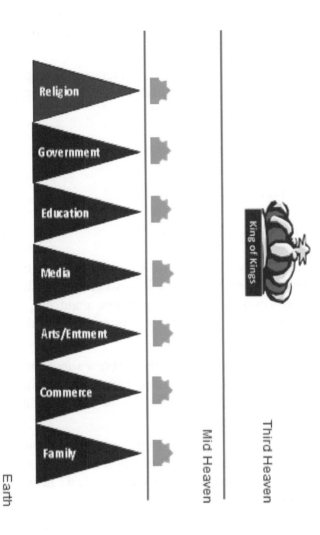

DIAGRAM 2 – The Heavenly Realms

Explanation of Diagram 2

At this point please refer to diagram 2. Each of the diagrams will build on the previous one and illustrate how the different aspects fit together.

In diagram 2 we have added a diagrammatic representation of the different levels of authority within the spiritual realm. These are represented by the:

- Third Heaven
- Mid Heaven
- Earth

The Plurality of Heaven

There are several words in scripture that are translated into English as "heaven". There is however one main one used in the Old Testament Hebrew and one main one used in New Testament Greek. The Hebrew is *samayim* and the Greek is *ouranos*.

It is interesting to note that the Hebrew *samayim* is plural, and that the Greek *ouranos* is also often used in the plural. This means that in both in the Old and the New Testaments, heaven is referred to in the plural.

It is of further interest in the context of our subject, to understand that the word "heaven" be it in the singular or the plural, can be used of either the "physical" heaven, or indeed the "spiritual" abode of God and angels.

The physical heavens are referred to in the very first verse of the Bible, and these represent the "firmament" which is the physical and visible sky above us.

God's Fivefold Strategy

In the beginning God created the heavens and the earth.

Genesis 1:1

This same plural use is continued in the following verses that relate to the unfolding of God's plan of creation.

Thus the heavens and the earth were completed in all their vast array. By the seventh day God had finished the work he had been doing; so on the seventh day he rested from all his work. And God blessed the seventh day and made it holy, because on it he rested from all the work of creating that he had done.

This is the account of the heavens and the earth when they were created.

When the LORD God made the earth and the heavens – and no shrub of the field had yet appeared on the earth and no plant of the field had yet sprung up, for the LORD God had not sent rain on the earth and there was no man to work the ground, but streams came up from the earth and watered the whole surface of the ground – the LORD God formed the man from the dust of the ground and breathed into his nostrils the breath of life, and the man became a living being.

Genesis 2:1-7

The physical heavens seem to have held great fascination throughout the history of mankind, and have been the source of untold legend and mystic enquiry. Even today mankind continues to "go where no man has gone before" in an attempt to unravel the mystery of space.

Moses described the heavens as the "storehouse of God" in Deuteronomy 28. In this way he made the connection between the physical, natural "heavens" and the spiritual blessings to be received from Almighty God.

In addition to the physical heavens, there is a weight of scripture that refers to the "heavens" or "heavenly places" as the eternal dwelling place of God. As God is "spirit" [12] and existed in eternity before the physical heavens were created, the implication here is that of a spiritual entity rather than a physical location.

Of the many instances where God is referred to as being "in heaven" almost certainly the one most commonly expressed is contained in Matthew where Jesus gives instructions to His disciples regarding prayer.

> *Our Father in heaven hallowed be your name,*
> *your kingdom come, your will be done on earth*
> *as it is in heaven.*
>
> Matthew 6:9-10

Third Heaven

Early tradition within a cross section of spirituality contains reference to some form of multiple heavens. There are many other non-Biblical books and writings that also describe the layers. This model was still in use in the Middle Ages (1400s AD) when Dante wrote of the various levels of heaven and hell.

The Apostle Paul when writing to the Corinthian church, most probably with reference to his conversion experience, made reference to a "third heaven".

---

[12] John 4:24

God's Fivefold Strategy

I must go on boasting. Although there is nothing to be gained, I will go on to visions and revelations from the Lord. I know a man in Christ who fourteen years ago was caught up to the third heaven. Whether it was in the body or out of the body I do not know – God knows. And I know that this man – whether in the body or apart from the body I do not know, but God knows – was caught up to paradise. He heard inexpressible things, things that man is not permitted to tell.

2 Corinthians 12:1-4

This concept of different levels in the multiple heavens is further reflected in the epistles of Paul. In his writings the Apostle Paul appears to suggest some correlation between the various heavens and the hierarchy of spiritual authority.

I pray also that the eyes of your heart may be enlightened in order that you may know the hope to which he has called you, the riches of his glorious inheritance in the saints, and his incomparably great power for us who believe. That power is like the working of his mighty strength, which he exerted in Christ when he raised him from the dead and seated him at his right hand in the heavenly realms, far above all rule and authority, power and dominion, and every title that can be given, not only in the present age but also in the one to come. And God placed all things under his feet and appointed him to be head over everything for the church, which is his body, the fullness of him who fills everything in every way.

Ephesians 1:18-23

The apostle further develops this concept of differing levels of authority in the hierarchies of heaven when describing the role of the church in God's eternal plan.

> *...and to make plain to everyone the administration of this mystery, which for ages past was kept hidden in God, who created all things. His intent was that now, through the church, the manifold wisdom of God should be made known to the rulers and authorities in the heavenly realms, according to his eternal purpose which he accomplished in Christ Jesus our Lord.*
>
> Ephesians 3:9-11

Spiritual Forces in Heavenly Places

The underlying premise in the Apostle Paul's writings that heaven contains various degrees and levels of spiritual authority and powers, is further endorsed later in Ephesians when he writes with regard to the ongoing spiritual conflict between the disciple of Christ, and the spiritual powers of darkness.

> *Finally, be strong in the Lord and in his mighty power. Put on the full armour of God so that you can take your stand against the devil's schemes. For our struggle is not against flesh and blood, but against the rulers, against the authorities, against the powers of this dark world and against the spiritual forces of evil in the heavenly realms. Therefore put on the full armour of God, so that when the day of evil comes, you may be able to stand your ground, and after you have done everything, to stand.*
>
> Ephesian 6:10-13

The subject of heaven is fascinating and cries out for a deeper study than this brief overview, however, the purpose of this section has been to lay a foundation of understanding in order to explain the depiction in diagram 2 of three levels of heaven.

For the purposes of exploring God's Fivefold Strategy we shall express heaven in terms of levels of spiritual authority.

Level 1 – Earth

This represents the environment of the natural world. It is where our earthly humanity is expressed and where the nations of the world exist.

Level 2 – The Mid Heaven

This represents the abode of the spiritual powers and authorities that are in conflict with the Kingdom of God. It is through these spiritual powers and authorities that Jesus ascended in His resurrection.

Level 3 – The Third Heaven

This is the abode of God and His angels. It contains the throne of God which is the seat of ultimate authority. It is the place where Jesus sits as King of Kings and Lord of Lords. It is also the place in which those in Christ have also been seated in terms of spiritual authority.

The extent of this authority and the way in which it can be exercised will be considered under the section entitled *Invasion*.

Crowns

In diagram 2 the spiritual authorities in the second and third heavens are represented by crowns. Reigning above all things is the "King of Kings and Lord of Lords". This is the position of the resurrected Christ who rules and reigns over all creation.

The earth is the Lord's, and everything in it.

1 Corinthians 10:26

The crowns in the mid heaven correspond to the spiritual powers that have been established over each of the seven mountains of influence. How they have gained authority and how they can be deposed will be explained in a later chapter under the heading *Invasion*.

We shall now proceed to build up the different sections of God's Strategic Plan. Each phase will be indicated as incremental additions to diagram 1 which will ultimately develop into a consolidated representation of God's Fivefold Strategy.

20

Stage One - Identity

Who am I? Where do I come from? What are my roots? These are questions that most people will ask at some point in their lives. The growing fascination of research into family trees has been greatly boosted by the powerful search engines available through the internet, but has, as its ultimate goal, the desire to be reconnected to our roots.

The Bible has several passages that present very detailed genealogies. In fact the term "son of" appears 1136 times in the New International Version, and the term "daughter of" some 131 times. This makes over 1260 occasions when not only is the name of the individual recorded, but also reference is made to their heritage.

Knowing our heritage gives us a deep sense of identity, and it is through knowing our identity that we gain some deeper sense of our destiny in life.[13] A study of the spiritual journeys of our ancestors can bring much insight into the issues encountered in our own lives.

---

[13] The subject of destiny is covered in *Adoption and Destiny* by the same author. ISBN 978-190792-905-2

For many years my wife, Jane, and I have been privileged to serve the Body of Christ in bringing greater freedom into people's lives. Freedom that releases many hindrances, either spiritually, emotionally, or indeed, physically that have been permitted to come down through the family line.

If Christians are to fulfil their God given destiny in their lives then it is vital that they gain a deep sense of their true identity in Christ. This identity in Christ not only deals with the past in individual lives, but cuts off the believer from any generational baggage.

Identity in Christ

Although much can be written on the subject of identity in Christ from a personal perspective, the focus of this section will be to emphasise the spiritual positioning of the believer.

Perhaps one of the most releasing Scriptures with regard to the believer's identity in Christ is found in the Apostle Paul's second letter to the church at Corinth.

> *So from now on we regard no one from a worldly point of view. Though we once regarded Christ in this way, we do so no longer. Therefore, if anyone is in Christ, he is a new creation; the old has gone, the new has come!*
>
> 2 Corinthians 5:16-17

Whatever we were, whatever our natural heritage, whatever has happened to us in our lives before Christ, is to be considered past and gone. There is a newness and a freedom that comes through faith in Christ which transcends all the past tragedies and traumas.

Testimonies abound of the life transforming power of the new birth in Christ. It is one of the most rewarding benefits of the ministry to see the wonderful grace of God change the individual believer from one degree of glory to the next.

This on-going transformation occurs as the new believer in Christ seeks to live in accordance with the Word of God and be continually empowered by the Spirit of God.

Personally I have known the reality of Paul's admonition to the believers at Ephesus regarding the day to day experience of the infilling of the Holy Spirit.

> *Do not get drunk on wine, which leads to debauchery. Instead, be filled with the Spirit.*

> Ephesians 5:18

It should be noted here that the tense of the verb is in the imperative and this would indicate that this is not some add on optional extra, but a direct command for all Christians.

The Greek language uses the present tense which also rules out any once-for-all reception of the Spirit but advises us to look to a continuous replenishment. Often this is referred to as *"be being filled"* or *"go on being filled"*.

Another very interesting point to note here is that the verb is "passive". This means that this infilling cannot be "produced by self effort" but rather making oneself available to God in such a way that would release the Holy Spirit into our lives as an ongoing experience.

Positional Identity

As the focus of this book is more on God's Fivefold Strategy rather than on the transformation of the individual believer, we shall now consider the concept of "Positional Identity".

In an earlier chapter [14] we discovered that an understanding of the principle of "Positional Authority and the Church" is vital if we are to see the Kingdom of God impact the world in these last days.

We saw how the individual believer, and therefore the church, has been raised up and seated with God in the heavenly places. This is a most remarkable truth, the practical application of which needs to be clearly understood and applied.

Head, Body and Feet

The Apostle Paul paints a very interesting picture with regards to the risen Lord Jesus and the church.

> *And God placed all things under his feet and appointed him to be head over everything for the church, which is his body, the fullness of him who fills everything in every way.*

> Ephesians 1:22-23

In this picture he refers to Jesus as the "head" of the church, which in turn is referred to as the "body". The reference to "all things" being under the feet would therefore imply that the "all things" are also under the church, as indeed the feet are the lowest part of the body.

---

[14] Chapter 8 – *Positional Authority and the Church*

Stage One – Identity

In ancient times it was customary for a conquering king to place his "foot" upon the head or the neck of a defeated enemy, to proclaim victory and authority. We read about this practice several times in the Old Testament.

> *Joshua said, "Open the mouth of the cave and bring those five kings out to me." So they brought the five kings out of the cave--the kings of Jerusalem, Hebron, Jarmuth, Lachish and Eglon. When they had brought these kings to Joshua, he summoned all the men of Israel and said to the army commanders who had come with him, "Come here and put your feet on the necks of these kings." So they came forward and placed their feet on their necks.*

Joshua 10:22-24

This represents total authority on the one hand by the victor, and total submission on the other hand by the vanquished. It is also what is implied by the use of the term "footstool".

> *Exalt the LORD our God and worship at his footstool; he is holy.*

Psalm 99:5

> *The LORD says to my Lord: "Sit at my right hand   until I make your enemies a footstool for your feet."*

Psalm 110:1

If we are to acknowledge the validity of Paul's picture of the church as the "body" of which Christ is the "head" then we will also need to acknowledge the positional identity of the church.

This positional identity is indicated in diagram 3.

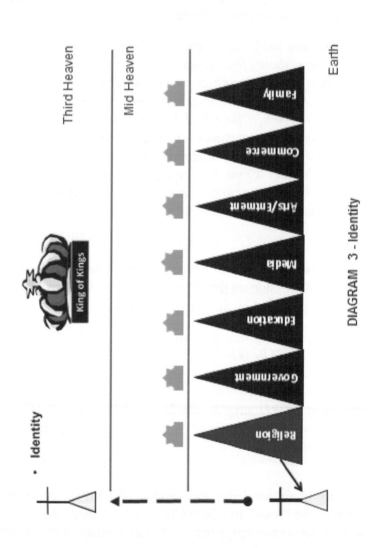

DIAGRAM 3 - Identity

Explanation of Diagram 3

We now add an element to the earlier diagrams. In this case the cross mounted on top of the triangle represents the "True Church". This term is used to make a distinction between the "Mountain of Religion" which includes all of the world's religions, and the church made up of true disciples of Jesus Christ.

The term "True Church" is not meant to be disrespectful to any specific group or denomination but seeks rather to emphasise the positional identity of those who are truly born again of the Spirit and who constitute the "Body of Christ".

The word used in the Greek language for church is *ekklesia* which literally means "called out". In truth the New Covenant church of which Jesus is the "head" is comprised of those who have been "called out" from the way of the world, and "gathered together" unto Jesus.

In being gathered "to Jesus", the church retains its 'physical' existence on the earth, but also, in being "raised with Jesus", the church is given a spiritual position in the Third Heaven. It is this identity in the Third Heaven that the church must come to fully appreciate if it is to fulfill its role on the earth in this age.

If the Third Heaven represents the abode, or dwelling place of God, and the church is raised up and seated there with Christ, then that is a spiritual position akin to that from which Adam was rejected as a result of rebellion.

Although the complete restoration of all things must await the Second Coming of Christ, the church in "this age" represents the first fruits of that fullness, and as such has a degree of "representation" of the Kingdom of God on the earth.

It is from this Third Heaven position that the church is to exercise its spiritual authority over the principalities and powers in the "lower'" Mid Heaven. How this is achieved will be examined under the fourth stage of God's Fivefold Strategy under the chapter headed *Invasion.*

21

Stage Two - Intimacy

Having identified the True Church as being established with an identity that embodies an existence both on earth and in the Third Heaven at one and the same time, it is now appropriate to consider the second stage of God's Fivefold Strategy, that of "Intimacy".

It is by being established in this identity that the church is brought into an experience of relationship, that is very different to the traditional concept of God as a far distant and severe judge.

The word "Intimacy" is one that depicts a close and personal relationship whereby each party in that relationship share at the deepest level.

Diagram 4 shows that intimacy is a direct benefit of the church's identity within the Third Heaven. At the very core of the Christian message is the restoration of such a relationship between God and mankind that was broken by Adam's rebellion.

Humanity was created by God, and indeed in God's likeness. Not that mankind could ever aspire to be God, but that the very essence of man was created in such a way as it could identify with and relate to, Almighty God.

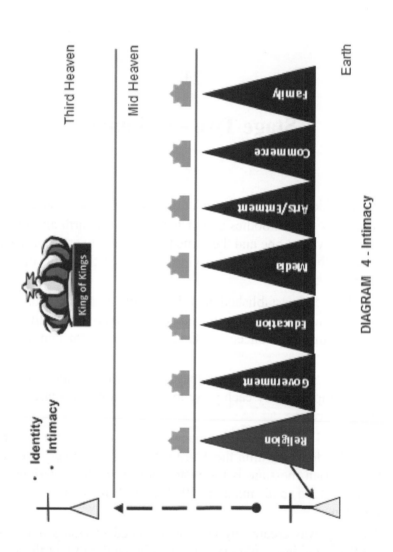

DIAGRAM 4 - Intimacy

Stage Two – Intimacy

God created man in his own image, in the image of God he created him; male and female he created them.

Genesis 1:27

God created mankind to be "with Him" and to fellowship with Him. He walked and talked with Adam in the garden in the cool of the day.[15]

Adam was entrusted with all responsibility to oversee creation as God's representative. He was given this authority within the context of a close and intimate relationship. Sadly the story of his rebellion is well recorded and humanity has reaped the consequences to this very day.

Even after God had banished Adam and Eve from the intimacy of His presence, God did not cease to love and care for His creation. The very act of banishing Adam from the Garden of Eden was in order that Adam could not have access to the "Tree of Life" and thereby live for eternity as a rebellious and fallen sinner with no hope of reconciliation.

And the LORD God said, "The man has now become like one of us, knowing good and evil. He must not be allowed to reach out his hand and take also from the tree of life and eat, and live forever." So the LORD God banished him from the Garden of Eden to work the ground from which he had been taken. After he drove the man out, he placed on the east side of the Garden of Eden cherubim and a flaming sword flashing back and forth to guard the way to the tree of life.

Genesis 3:22-24

---

[15] Genesis 3:8

From that moment, God set in motion a plan of reconciliation that would be fulfilled through the person of Jesus Christ of Nazareth. It is through Jesus that mankind can be forgiven of the consequence of sin, be reconciled with God, and restored to that place of love and intimacy.

Intimacy in the Desert

Long before Jesus appeared however, God revealed His desire to relate to mankind, not as some distant and thunderous deity, but as an intimate benefactor.

In Exodus we read the history of Israel in the wilderness and perhaps one of the sweetest verses in that whole account is found in chapter 25 and verse 8.

> *Then have them make a sanctuary for me, and I will dwell among them.*
>
> Exodus 25:8

God's heart was at the beginning, a heart desiring intimacy. Generations later His heart had not changed. The "Tabernacle" was to be a visual representation of the salvation that was to become available in Christ. Its construction charted the way from obscurity to intimacy.

It reflected the journey through the place of sacrifice at the altar, to the place of washing and cleansing at the brazen laver. From there the priest could enter through the "curtain" into the Holy of Holies where he would find the light of the golden lampstand, the fellowship of the table of shew bread, and the aroma of the altar of incense at the door to the Most Holy Place.

It was in the Most Holy Place, or the Holy of Holies that the Shekinah glory of the presence of Almighty God shone resplendent, lighting up the darkness of the shrouded tent. It was here that the High Priest would experience the intimacy of the Holy presence. It was here that the Ark of the Covenant stood. It was here that the Mercy Seat heralded the heart of God in forgiveness. What a glorious foretaste of all that would be achieved by Jesus at Calvary.

The principles of the Tabernacle in the wilderness were later to be replicated in much more splendour in the Temple of Solomon. Although the grandeur far exceeded anything else, the typology of access to God remained the same.

It was in this temple as Jesus "gave up His spirit" on Calvary, that the curtain between the Holy Place and the Holy of Holies was torn in two from top to bottom.[16] This was an indication that the "veil of separation" between God and man had now been destroyed and God was again calling His beloved back to intimacy.

Jesus and Intimacy

When it became time for Jesus to begin His ministry and call out His disciples, we read that He first called them "to" Himself and then to a ministry.

> *As Jesus was walking beside the Sea of Galilee, he saw two brothers, Simon called Peter and his brother Andrew. They were casting a net into the lake, for they were fishermen. "Come, follow me," Jesus said, "and I will make you fishers of men." At once they left their nets and followed him.*
>
> Matthew 4:18-20

---

[16] Matthew 27:51; Mark 15:38; Luke 223:45

Ever before He commissioned them to "Go" He invited them to "Come". The twelve men that Jesus called to be His disciples were to live in "intimate" fellowship with Him for the next three years. These were the ones He called to be "with" Him in a much closer way than the rest of the multitudes that followed Jesus wherever He went. In fact much later, after the death of Jesus, the disciples were to be recognized as the men who had been "with Jesus".

> *When they saw the courage of Peter and John and realized that they were unschooled, ordinary men, they were astonished and they took note that these men had been with Jesus.*

> Acts 4:13

Possibly the most intense expression of intimacy is found in what has become known as the "High Priestly" prayer of Jesus. This is found in John chapter 17 and verse three is particularly interesting in this respect.

> *Father, the time has come. Glorify your Son, that your Son may glorify you. For you granted him authority over all people that he might give eternal life to all those you have given him.*

> John 17:1-2

Verse two refers to the granting of eternal life, the very thing withheld from Adam. Jesus then proceeds to give an indication of what this eternal life entails.

> *Now this is eternal life: that they may know you, the only true God, and Jesus Christ, whom you have sent.*

> John 17:3

The word used here in the text for *"know"* is extremely revealing with regard to the idea of intimacy with God. The Greek word is *ginosko* and relates, not just to the accumulation of accumulated facts 'about' God, but rather a deep and intimate understanding of the person 'of' God. It is the same word used to convey the essence of an intimate relationship between a man and a woman. Jesus develops this sense of intimacy as He continues to pray.

> *My prayer is not for them alone. I pray also for those who will believe in me through their message, that all of them may be one, Father, just as you are in me and I am in you. May they also be in us so that the world may believe that you have sent me. I have given them the glory that you gave me, that they may be one as we are one: I in them and you in me. May they be brought to complete unity to let the world know that you sent me and have loved them even as you have loved me.*

> *Father, I want those you have given me to be with me where I am, and to see my glory, the glory you have given me because you loved me before the creation of the world.*

> *Righteous Father, though the world does not know you, I know you, and they know that you have sent me. I have made you known to them, and will continue to make you known in order that the love you have for me may be in them and that I myself may be in them."*

Here, the heart of Father God for intimacy with His creation is revealed through the words of Jesus. There is no more intense expression of intimacy than to be "indwelt" with Jesus.

The Father Heart of God

Although God's heart has always been that of a father, the past twenty years or so has seen the Holy Spirit raising the awareness of the church to this great message.

In the mid 1990s the outbreak of revival in Toronto was energised greatly by the deep revelation of God's love and of the Father's heart. Whatever one's initial reaction to the so called "excesses" of those early days, the long lasting fruit bears witness to the integrity of that revival to know the deep love of God and to give it away.

The church at large should thank God for such folk as John and Carol Arnott and team at Toronto Airport Christian Fellowship,[17] The late Jack Frost was also at the forefront of this reawakening to God as a loving and intimate father and his books are well worth reading to this day.

Another ministry that has blessed many people is that of Dr Mark Stibbe. Mark, until recently, was a very successful Anglican vicar, following Rev David Pytches at Chorleywood in England. Mark was in fact, adopted as a child and his story of how the revelation of spiritual adoption and the Father heart of God impacted his own life makes inspirational reading. Mark is now heading up a powerful ministry, *The Father's House Trust,* and is reaching out to the world with the "Father's Embrace".

---

[17] Renamed in 2011 as 'Catch the Fire – Toronto'

Intimacy and Identity

The importance of intimacy cannot be overstated. It is through the restoration of relationship between fallen mankind and Father God that we regain our sense of identity and purpose.

In the parable of the Prodigal Son in Luke 15, we learn that God is represented by the father and fallen mankind by the prodigal son. It is through returning back from isolation to the intimacy of the father that the profligate son regained a sense of identity and dignity.

> *The son said to him, `Father, I have sinned against heaven and against you. I am no longer worthy to be called your son. '*
>
> *But the father said to his servants, `Quick! Bring the best robe and put it on him. Put a ring on his finger and sandals on his feet. Bring the fattened calf and kill it. Let's have a feast and celebrate. For this son of mine was dead and is alive again; he was lost and is found.' So they began to celebrate."*

> Luke 15:21-24

Restoration to the father's house brought with it a return to the father's blessings. It also returned the prodigal back to his true identity and dignity as a son of the family line.

The older brother on the other hand, although never leaving the family home, had never really enjoyed a sense of intimacy with his father. If intimacy is lacking then all our endeavours will be reduced to hard work and toil. The older brother's identity was defined by "what he did" rather than "who he was".

Many well meaning Christians today struggle with "burn out" in their life and ministry as they "work hard" in an endeavour to gain some sense of identity and purpose. This was never God's plan. It is only through our sense of acceptance and intimacy that we can ever really gain our sense of true identity and purpose.

It seems therefore more than appropriate to suggest that the first two stages of realizing God's Fivefold Strategy is to appreciate and experience the inseparable joint restoration of "identity and intimacy" with our Heavenly Father.

From this sense of identity and intimacy the church can then truly begin to function in the next stage of God's Fivefold Strategy and that is of "Intercession".

22

Stage Three – Intercession

There seems to be for some a cloud of mystery about "intercession" as if it were the sole province of a special breed of 'super-saints'! It seems to have been sidelined by the church and given over to a select group of specialists who gather behind closed doors to do some special business with God. The truth is, in fact, very different.

The term "intercede" simply means to act as a "mediator" between two estranged parties in order to end a dispute or broken relationship.

In this way Jesus is declared in the New Testament to be the "mediator of the new covenant"[18] and the only mediator between God and men[19].

However there is a calling on the church in the New Testament to take on the ministry of "intercession". As we fully appreciate our "identity" as being raised with Christ, and thereby enjoying the great privilege of close fellowship and

---

[18] Hebrews 9:15;12:24
[19] 1 Timothy 2:5

"intimacy" with God, we shall begin to catch a revelation of the uniqueness of the church in this role.

The fact that the "true church" is "bi-located" presents a unique opportunity to be effective as intercessors. Our earthly positioning means that we can truly engage with, and identify with, the people around us. We can be involved with the various "ethnos" groupings with which we interact in our everyday lives.

The privileged position in Christ that has exalted the church into the Third Heaven means that it has open access to the throne of God. This means that the church has the greatest potential of anyone else on earth, or indeed in heaven, to be powerfully effective in the ministry of intercession. With one hand the church holds onto the people, and with the other, holds onto God.

New Testament Priesthood

In many ways the role of the priests in the Old Testament gives a pattern of the ministry of intercession. The priests were called to minister in the tabernacle and the temple as those who would "represent God before the people and represent the people before God".

The priests would receive the offering from the people according to the situation, and then serve that as a sacrifice at the altar of God on behalf of the people. The following New Testament Scripture calls the church to a similar priestly role.

> *But you are a chosen people, a royal priesthood, a holy nation, a people belonging to God, that you may declare the praises of him who called you out of darkness into his wonderful light. Once you were not a people, but now you are*

the people of God; once you had not received
mercy, but now you have received mercy.

1 Peter 2:9-10

As a chosen people and a holy nation belonging to God, the church is called to carry out this "go-between" ministry of intercession. The apostle Paul makes this point when writing his first letter to Timothy.

I urge, then, first of all, that requests, prayers,
intercession and thanksgiving be made for
everyone – for kings and all those in authority,
that we may live peaceful and quiet lives in all
godliness and holiness. This is good, and
pleases God our Saviour, who wants all men to
be saved and to come to a knowledge of the
truth.

1 Timothy 2:1-4

Intercession is much more than simply praying, but carries with it a sense of earnest endeavour and passionate pleading. It requires the intercessor to "identify" with the need at a heart level and then to "plead the case with passion" before the throne of God.

Abraham interceded for Sodom

There is a wonderful account in Genesis 18 of how Abraham pleaded with God for the city of Sodom. The situation in Sodom was desperate at that time with all sorts of ungodliness running rife throughout the city. Abraham's heart was to see the righteous saved and to this end he entered into a fascinating dialogue with God. As you read this account ask yourself this question. "Am I as bold and persistent in intercession as Abraham?" If not, then why not?

> *The men turned away and went toward Sodom, but Abraham remained standing before the LORD. Then Abraham approached him and said: "Will you sweep away the righteous with the wicked? What if there are fifty righteous people in the city? Will you really sweep it away and not spare the place for the sake of the fifty righteous people in it? Far be it from you to do such a thing − -to kill the righteous with the wicked, treating the righteous and the wicked alike. Far be it from you! Will not the Judge of all the earth do right?"*
>
> Genesis 18:22-25

It almost seems highly impertinent for Abraham to address God in such a manner, but Abraham was passionate and passion drives us forward into persistence. If you stop praying for situations before you see the answer then press on with passionate persistence until you see the answer. Take Abraham's lead here.

> *The LORD said, "If I find fifty righteous people in the city of Sodom, I will spare the whole place for their sake."*
>
> *Then Abraham spoke up again: "Now that I have been so bold as to speak to the Lord, though I am nothing but dust and ashes, what if the number of the righteous is five less than fifty? Will you destroy the whole city because of five people?"*

152

Stage Three – Intercession

"If I find forty-five there," he said, "I will not destroy it."

Genesis 18:25-28

Abraham continued to press in on God, almost bargain with God, for the sake of the righteous in the city. The bargaining continued in the following verses until Abraham managed to get an agreement with God for the sake of "ten" righteous.[20] The fact that God destroyed the city of Sodom is indicative of the total depravity of the people, and the distinct lack of "ten" righteous people.

The Boldness of Intercession

Most people will be familiar with what has become known as The Lord's Prayer. In fact it was not the Lord Jesus who was to pray this prayer, but rather the prayer was a model for His disciples to use. The prayer of Jesus in John chapter 17, would perhaps be better annotated as The Lord's Prayer.

However, immediately after instructing the disciples on the way of prayer in Luke 11, Jesus proceeded to illustrate the necessity of boldness when "interceding" on behalf of others.

Then he said to them, "Suppose one of you has a friend, and he goes to him at midnight and says, `Friend, lend me three loaves of bread, because a friend of mine on a journey has come to me, and I have nothing to set before him.'

"Then the one inside answers, `Don't bother me. The door is already locked, and my children are with me in bed. I can't get up and give you

---

[20] Genesis 18:29-32

*anything.' I tell you, though he will not get up
and give him the bread because he is his friend,
yet because of the man's boldness[21] he will get
up and give him as much as he needs.*

Luke 11:5-8

It seems that God really loves us to be persistent and bold in our intercession. It is clear throughout Scripture that God honours "faith" but faith is passionate and faith is persistent.

If we truly have the heart of God for a situation, then we will not give up before we see the answer. We will press in, we will persevere, we will literally move heaven and earth until the answer comes.

The Necessity of Intercession

There is a verse in Ezekiel that reverberates with tragic consequences for the land of Judah. At the time of the prophet Ezekiel there was deliberate disobedience to the Mosaic Covenant throughout the land, both in the people and in the leaders especially the recent kings Manasseh and Jehoiakim along with prince Zedekiah. Each of these rulers had abused their position and misused their power, and each one had broken the explicit prohibitions of the Mosaic covenant.[22]

A brief overview of the situation in those days will clearly display a similarity to many western democracies at this current time. The "Seven Mountains" of influence in our nations in the main have much in common with the ungodliness in the nation of Judah at that time.

---

[21] The *New Living Translation* has the phrase 'shameless persistence' which seems very appropriate in this case.

[22] cf. 2Ki 21:16; 24:4

The rulers ignored the rightful place and authority of parents, thus destroying the home and the family and socially these leaders were taking advantage of the helpless. Their indifference to God and His righteousness caused them to permit all manner of ungodly activities among the people. They disregarded the Sabbaths, and broke many of the requirements of the Mosaic Covenant and the precepts of their God. They permitted an over-riding sense of dishonour to pervade the nation and sexual immorality abounded.

This was not simply a matter of neglect, but rather a definite act of rebellion in that, instead of enacting their holy practices they engaged in heathen rituals. This caused God to declare His displeasure with them.

> *You have forgotten me, declares the Sovereign LORD."*
>
> Ezekiel 22:12

Having made that solemn declaration about the people, God then proceeds to make what must be one of the most tragic statements in the Bible.

> *I looked for a man among them who would build up the wall and stand before me in the gap on behalf of the land so I would not have to destroy it, but I found none. So I will pour out my wrath on them and consume them with my fiery anger, bringing down on their own heads all they have done, declares the Sovereign LORD.*
>
> Ezekiel 22:30-31

God found no intercessor! God found not one single person who could "stand in the gap". Not one person who could be in touch with the people and in touch with God. No one who could build up the brokenness of the wall.

It was because God could not find even one, that He declares *"So I will pour out my wrath on them"*. What a tragedy!

Intercession Today

Praise God, today around the world there are many individuals and groups who are "standing in the gap" and passionately interceding for world situations. We give God thanks for these initiatives, and we should honour them and appreciate their endeavours. However "intercession" should not be the province of these specialists only, but an integrated part of the whole. This is the heart cry of the vision behind God's Fivefold Strategy.

Individuals and local church groups should be encouraged to see themselves in their true "identity" in Christ, in that "intimate" place with the Father and making that passionate connection between the brokenness of our world and the Throne Room of Heaven.

It is as we engage progressively with each aspect of the Fivefold Strategy, that we will be more effective in releasing the Kingdom of Heaven on the earth. The last part of this book will seek to pull together the different stages of the strategy and illustrate how every single believer, and every local church group, can make the difference in each of the "Seven Mountains" of influence in our communities.

Stage Three – Intercession

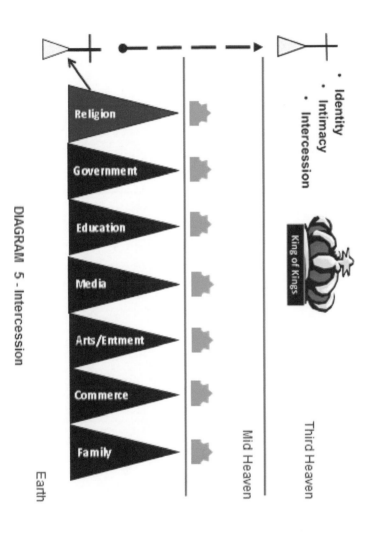

DIAGRAM 5 - Intercession

Earth

Mid Heaven

Third Heaven

Religion
Government
Education
Media
Arts/Entment
Commerce
Family

King of Kings

- Identity
- Intimacy
- Intercession

Kingdom and Culture

23

Stage Four – Invasion

Having seen how our "Identity" in Christ raises up the believer into that place of "Intimacy" and "Intercession" on behalf of our communities, the next stage in God's Fivefold Strategy is one of "Invasion". It is imperative at this point that the reader appreciates the use of the word "Invasion" in the context of God's Fivefold Strategy.

Remember that stages one, two and three have been a progression from earth to Heaven. From living subject to the "ruler of this world", to being part of the Body of Christ, seated above all principalities and powers in the heavenly places.

So far the focus of attention has been on the relationship between the believer and God. Now the attention changes to that of the relationship between the believer and the principalities and powers that govern the Seven Mountains of Influence. These are indicated by the crowns in diagram 6.

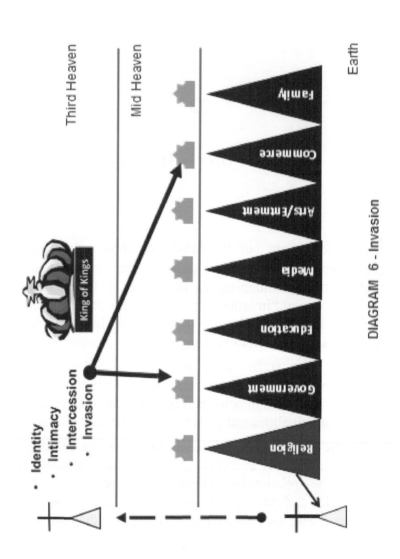

Third Heaven

Mid Heaven

Earth

- Identity
- Intimacy
- Intercession
- Invasion

King of Kings

Invasion

Religion

Government

Education

Media

Arts/Entmnt

Commerce

Family

DIAGRAM 6 - Invasion

Why Invasion?

The term invasion is used in this context to suggest the forceful removal of one ruling principality and the establishment of another. In recent years the subject of regime change has been brought to prominence through world politics with the removal of Saddam Hussein in Iraq and the uprisings in other Middle Eastern states.

Invasion consists of much more than military victories on the battlefields. Invasion is much more than aerial bombardment that demolishes the land and destroys armies on the ground. Invasion requires the establishment of the rule of law and the reconstruction of the constituencies of state.

The use of the word in the context of the Fivefold Strategy refers to the engagement in spiritual warfare by the true church against the spiritual forces of darkness that have been allowed to establish strongholds over the seven mountains of influence.

Footholds and Strongholds

A "foothold" is a place of relative stability from which further progress may be accomplished. For a rock climber, it may be the smallest of ledges on the rock face, for a political party it may be a small majority in a local election, whilst for the devil, it may be that one small weakness in our lives that gives him access.

In his letter to the church at Ephesus the Apostle Paul encourages the believers not to give the devil such a foothold. He places great emphasis on preventing even the smallest of ledges to be carved on the rock face of our lives.

> *Therefore each of you must put off falsehood and speak truthfully to his neighbour, for we are all members of one body. "In your anger do not sin" : Do not let the sun go down while you are still angry, and do not give the devil a foothold. He who has been stealing must steal no longer, but must work, doing something useful with his own hands, that he may have something to share with those in need.*

> Ephesians 4:25-28

Please be advised to read the sections of scripture before and after the verses quoted. It will be seen that by submitting to the way of life that was common-place prior to salvation, it is possible to give the devil a "foothold" in one's life from which he can make progress.

The "foothold" becomes a "stronghold" when it is reinforced, and it is reinforced through repetition. Whenever a Christian chooses to reject the will of God in any given situation and therefore, by default, chooses to give the devil more of a foothold, that foothold is reinforced by repeated acts of disobedience. If this becomes a repeated pattern then it is not long before the devil has a stronghold in that area of the believer's life.

This is the principle that Paul was addressing in Romans 6.

> *What then? Shall we sin because we are not under law but under grace? By no means! Don't you know that when you offer yourselves to someone to obey him as slaves, you are slaves to the one whom you obey – whether you are slaves to sin, which leads to death, or to obedience, which leads to righteousness?*

> Romans 6:15-16

For part of my military career I served with the airborne forces. The particular role of the logistics squadron in which I served was to assist with the establishment of drop zones into which the main battalion would "drop".

This meant that an initial, small, advance party would be dropped into an area, locate a suitable site for the DZ and then proceed to prepare it, and mark it out to accommodate the battalion, or indeed the brigade.

This is a really good analogy of how the devil gains access to our lives. The initial access may be very small and go relatively unnoticed, but once established, it will prepare the ground for reinforcements of evil and destruction.

The Enemy

In any adversarial activity one of the major keys to success is to "know your enemy". To know his strengths and weakness, his size, his equipment, his behaviour patterns in certain circumstances, and so on. In sport, for example, teams spend hours of pre-match preparation watching films of the opponent's past matches in order to strategise and create the right tactics in order to maximise their relative strengths.

Scripture gives believers a wake up call to the strategies and tactics of the devil.

> *Be self-controlled and alert. Your enemy (adversary) the devil prowls around like a roaring lion looking for someone to devour. Resist him, standing firm in the faith.*
>
> 1 Peter 5:8

Kingdom and Culture

In the context of the Fivefold Strategy it is absolutely vital that
we understand the identity of the enemy. The adversary is not,
repeat not, the mountain, nor indeed the people within the
mountain of influence. The enemy is the spiritual principality
and power that is controlling the activities of that mountain.
This point must be understood, as much damage can be done
by well meaning, and passionate believers, if mistakes are
made here.

Increasingly we hear of the use of "human shields" in the many
war-torn lands around the world today. It is an age old tactic of
surrounding a specific "military" target with groups of innocent
civilians in the hope that the enemy will not attack the military
target for fear of killing the civilians. Although most world
leaders would not risk civilian deaths in such a case, there are
others for whom that situation would offer little restraint.

As we seek to engage with the enemy forces governing the
mountains of influence, we must identify both the enemy and
the innocent civilians so to speak. The Apostle Paul gives us a
clear insight into this situation in Ephesians chapter 6.

> *Finally, be strong in the Lord and in his mighty*
> *power. Put on the full armour of God so that*
> *you can take your stand against the devil's*
> *schemes. For our struggle is not against flesh*
> *and blood, but against the rulers, against the*
> *authorities, against the powers of this dark*
> *world and against the spiritual forces of evil in*
> *the heavenly realms. Therefore put on the full*
> *armor of God, so that when the day of evil*
> *comes, you may be able to stand your ground,*
> *and after you have done everything, to stand.*

Ephesians 6:10-13

It is important that the enemy is identified as the spiritual rulers, authorities, powers of this dark world, and the spiritual forces of evil in the heavenly realms. The enemy is not, repeat not, the mountains of influence, nor the people who inhabit them.

The Seven Nations in Canaan

There are some today who would make a direct comparison between the seven mountains of influence and the seven nations in Canaan that were to be defeated and displaced by Israel. Indeed it is true that the seven nations were to be driven out of Canaan in order for the people of God to take their rightful inheritance.

> *When the LORD your God brings you into the land you are entering to possess and drives out before you many nations – the Hittites, Girgashites, Amorites, Canaanites, Perizzites, Hivites and Jebusites, seven nations larger and stronger than you – and when the LORD your God has delivered them over to you and you have defeated them, then you must destroy them totally. Make no treaty with them, and show them no mercy. Do not intermarry with them. Do not give your daughters to their sons or take their daughters for your sons, for they will turn your sons away from following me to serve other gods, and the LORD's anger will burn against you and will quickly destroy you.*

> Deuteronomy 7:1-4

It is also true that the characteristics of these nations bears some resemblance to the ungodliness of the practices carried out in many of the spheres of influence within our society today. The warning given to remain clear of them and of their influence is indeed apposite for believers today.

However, with reference to the seven mountains of influence, we should not seek to completely destroy the mountain, but rather deal with the spiritual forces that control them. The verses immediately following in Deuteronomy give some guidelines here.

> *This is what you are to do to them: Break down their altars, smash their sacred stones, cut down their Asherah poles and burn their idols in the fire. For you are a people holy to the LORD your God. The LORD your God has chosen you out of all the peoples on the face of the earth to be his people, his treasured possession.*
>
> Deuteronomy 7:5-6

The "principle" of invasion is to destroy the spiritual strongholds without destroying the individual people that the devil is using as a "human shield". Remember that God loves people, Jesus came to save people, and the church is to reach people.

The process therefore of invasion, is to engage the controlling spiritual forces with the authority and power of our position in the Kingdom of God, whilst at the same time reaching the people with the love and compassion of God in Jesus.

If "regime change" is to be achieved in the seven mountains then not only does the might and authority of the ruling spiritual powers need to be neutralized, but the hearts and minds of the people need to be won. How this is achieved will be covered in Stage 5 of the Fivefold Strategy under the heading "Influence".

24

Spiritual Engagement

Having identified the enemy as the spiritual forces that control the seven mountains we shall now proceed to formulate a strategy that enables the believer and the church to unseat them from their place of authority.

Remember that the church is exalted with Christ far above every principality and power and as such has the authority to command the will of God and the Kingdom of God to be established in any given circumstance. Indeed this is the essence of the teaching of Jesus in Matthew 6. The Lord's Prayer is not so much a plea for God to do something, but rather an encouragement for the disciples of Jesus to make a prophetic declaration and command that the Kingdom of God be established and the will of God be done.

> *Our Father in heaven, hallowed be your name,*
> *Your kingdom come, Your will be done, on earth*
> *as it is in heaven.*

Matthew 6:9-10

The Kingdom of God was advancing through Jesus and the disciples were to continue in much the same way. Every time the word of God is proclaimed with signs and wonders the Kingdom of God advances.

The difficulty arises at this point, already discussed earlier with regard to the extent to which the fullness of the Kingdom can be expected in this "age."

The position held by this author is one that embraces the theology that the Kingdom "is here" but also that the kingdom "is coming". It accepts the positional authority of the church as the people of the Kingdom now, in this age, but also takes into account that we await the fullness in the "age to come", at the return of Jesus in glorious triumph. It is embracing the tension of the "now and not yet"!

Dominion theology implies that the fullness of the Kingdom of God has already come. It argues that the church is called to subdue the nations of the earth in this age and to impose Kingdom rule and legislation, even upon the unsaved and the ungodly. Although this theology has many attractive aspects, has great aspirations, and presents challenges indeed for us all to forcefully advance, care must be taken against the dangers of presumption.

Prophetic Declaration

The church is called to be a prophetic people and to make prophetic declarations to the principalities and powers of what the will of God is in any situation.

Satan is a defeated foe and must now obey the commands of his victor, Jesus. The church, as the Body of Christ, carries the mandate as ambassadors to make the decrees of heaven known to the principalities and powers in the heavens and also upon the earth. The verses in Ephesians chapter 3 give some indication of this responsibility.

> *Although I am less than the least of all God's people, this grace was given me: to preach to the Gentiles the unsearchable riches of Christ, and to make plain to everyone the administration of this mystery, which for ages past was kept hidden in God, who created all things. His intent was that now, through the church, the manifold wisdom of God should be made known to the rulers and authorities in the heavenly realms, according to his eternal purpose which he accomplished in Christ Jesus our Lord.*
>
> Ephesians 3:8-11

The Word of God declares the will of God, and as such should not only be prayed back to God by the church, but "proclaimed with authority" by the church as a government would declare a statute.

Binding and Loosing

Although the Apostle Peter had historical primacy with regard to the commission to bind and loose, both he and the other disciples can stand as paradigms for all believers in this age.

> *I will give you the keys of the kingdom of heaven; whatever you bind on earth will be bound in heaven, and whatever you loose on earth will be loosed in heaven.*
>
> Matthew 16:19

In this way the disciples, and believers thereafter, are given the power and authority to both bind and to loose with regard to Kingdom activities. To "bind" means to restrict activity, and conversely to "loose" means to permit activity. With regard to the spiritual powers and the Kingdom of God, believers are given the authority to restrict the activity of the demonic forces, and also to loose the power of the word of God and the Kingdom of God in any given situation. With regard to the principalities and powers that govern the seven mountains of influence, believers therefore have an authority to limit their activities.

How this is achieved is a matter of some debate among the different streams of theology. For some "binding" is a direct verbal assault in prayer upon the principalities and powers including a command for them to withhold any further influence over the person or situation. Certainly the centurion of Matthew 8 knew the power of a spoken command, and Jesus commended him for his great faith.

Others would see "binding" as being the result of surrendering to the will of God. In such cases of surrender the power of the principality is restricted by the act of obedience. It was through His absolute obedience to the will of God that Jesus could claim that the Satan and his forces had no power of Him at all.

> *I will not speak with you much longer, for the prince of this world is coming. He has no hold on me.*
>
> John 14:30

Jesus was free from any demonic footholds because of His total surrender to the Father. This principle also extends to any person or organisation that chooses to live by Kingdom principles. Living free from demonic influences is not so much as result of "shouting at the darkness" but rather much more a benefit of "walking in the light"!

Opposite Spirit

For many years my wife, Jane, and I have seen significant breakthroughs in difficult situations by "working in the opposite spirit".

This is simply the practice of discerning the demonic principality and power that is influencing a situation and sowing into it in exactly the opposite way. For example where there is a situation that is subject to a destructive spirit of division, then we would endeavour to sow into that situation harmony and peace. Where there is an oppressive influence of hatred, then we would seek to sow God's unending love.

In this way, instead of the foothold being reinforced and strengthened by continual submission to the demonic influence, a foothold of righteousness and life is established which when continually reinforced by repetition, becomes a Kingdom stronghold where the devil has no authority at all.

> *He has showed you, O man, what is good, and what does the LORD require of you? To act justly and to love mercy and to walk humbly with your God.*
>
> Micah 6:8

With regard to the seven mountains of influence, one of the most important and powerful tools of transformation is to empower those decision makers within the mountains to make righteous judgements and decisions. It is one thing for churches and groups of intercessors to engage in passionate prayer, taking authority in the heavenly places, and binding and loosing every demonic influence. That may seem good to some, and indeed does have a place in the whole scheme of things, but it is yet another thing to have Christians of integrity and influence, making the decisions that shape the culture.

Explanation of Diagram 6

As we have progressed through the stages of the Fivefold Strategy we have progressively added elements to the diagrams. In diagram 6 there are two arrows descending from the word Invasion onto the mountain of government and the mountain of commerce.

In fact these two arrows are indicative of what happens over each of the seven mountains. The two have been chosen simply to avoid over cluttering the diagram. The principles applied to these two mountains are to be applied to all seven. These arrows represent the activity of the church as outlined in this chapter, towards the spiritual forces over each of the mountains.

Discerning Spiritual Strongholds

In order to defeat the spiritual strongholds it is important to identify them. Although it is true that ultimately any spiritual power must bow to the victory of Jesus at Calvary, there is insight gained if they can be discerned and identified.

Discernment may come directly through the ministry of the Holy Spirit. It is often during times of passionate intercession that the Holy Spirit will bring insight and understanding as to the spiritual activity relative to the situation.

Alternatively, spiritual strongholds can be identified by the fruits they display. If there is "fruit" then somewhere there is a "root". This applies to individuals as well as corporations and in this case the mountains.

By their fruit you will recognize them. Do people pick grapes from thornbushes, or figs from thistles? Likewise every good tree bears good fruit, but a bad tree bears bad fruit. A good tree cannot bear bad fruit, and a bad tree cannot bear good fruit. Every tree that does not bear good fruit is cut down and thrown into the fire. Thus, by their fruit you will recognize them.

Matthew 7:16-20

On this point of observation, there is an interesting deliverance performed by Jesus in Matthew 18. A man brought his son to Jesus and explained what the symptoms were. Jesus drove out the demon and the boy was healed. The father explained the "fruit" and Jesus dealt with the "root".

When they came to the crowd, a man approached Jesus and knelt before him. "Lord, have mercy on my son," he said. "He has seizures and is suffering greatly. He often falls into the fire or into the water. I brought him to your disciples, but they could not heal him."

"O unbelieving and perverse generation," Jesus replied, "how long shall I stay with you? How long shall I put up with you? Bring the boy here to me." Jesus rebuked the demon, and it came out of the boy, and he was healed from that moment.

Matthew 17:14-18

The third method of discerning of spirits is through systematic research. With regard to the seven mountains one might look at the history of the mountain. Why was it established? How was

173

it established? What major historical events have influenced the development of the mountain?

For example there are aspects of the mountain of "Commerce" that were established on the slave trade. This was clearly rooted in manipulation, domination, murder, treachery, which if allowed to remain will influence decisions made today.

The recent international banking collapse was due to unbridled greed and avarice. Again some research into the banking industry would highlight times when these forces were permitted to enter and shape the future.

Identification Confession

Once the controlling principality has been identified it must be dealt with. At this point we must appreciate that the only power or authority the principality can exert is in the area that is not submitted to God.

Since Calvary the blood of Jesus cleanses from all sin in principle, but in practice, the blood of Jesus cleanses only the sin that is brought before Him in confession and repentance.

> *If we claim to have fellowship with him yet walk in the darkness, we lie and do not live by the truth. But if we walk in the light, as he is in the light, we have fellowship with one another, and the blood of Jesus, his Son, purifies us from all sin.*
>
> *If we claim to be without sin, we deceive ourselves and the truth is not in us. If we confess our sins, he is faithful and just and will forgive us our sins and purify us from all unrighteousness.*
>
> 1 John 1:6-9

Identification confession is the practice of someone who has a link with the problem, taking the responsibility of the sin upon themselves and repenting of the sin on behalf of all that has gone before.

A clear example of this in the Old Testament was when Nehemiah went before God on behalf of the leaders of Israel who had permitted Jerusalem to fall into the hands of their enemies and become a reproach before God.

> *O LORD, God of heaven, the great and awesome God, who keeps his covenant of love with those who love him and obey his commands, let your ear be attentive and your eyes open to hear the prayer your servant is praying before you day and night for your servants, the people of Israel. I confess the sins we Israelites, including myself and my father's house, have committed against you. We have acted very wickedly toward you. We have not obeyed the commands, decrees and laws you gave your servant Moses.*

Nehemiah 1:5-7

Nehemiah identified himself with the failure of his ancestors and his pleas were accepted by God. As a result God gave him favour with the king and the king released him for a time to rebuild Jerusalem and also blessed him with letters of authority and the wherewithal in men and equipment to see the job completed.

As Christians get serious about taking on the responsibility for the failures of our ancestors to retain a Godly perspective in the Seven Mountains, and then to confess and repent, the grip of the controlling principalities and powers is broken.

This leaves the way open for others to enter into those mountains and begin the rebuilding process. This is achieved through the next stage in the Fivefold Strategy, that of Influence.

25

Stage Five – Influence

Having identified the first four steps of God's Fivefold Strategy we now move onto the fifth and last, that of influence.

It is important to appreciate the progressive nature of the strategy at this point. Each step builds upon the previous one. It is through appreciating our new "Identity" in Christ at salvation that we can understand our place of "Intimacy" with the Father in the Kingdom of God.

It is at that place of intimacy that we gain some insight into the heart of the Father and His love and compassion for the world He created. It is only as we gain His heart, that we can truly intercede with passion. Our connectedness with the world in which we live, and our connectedness to the Father, gives us a unique opportunity to fulfil our role as priests unto our God.

It is as we intercede that we gain discernment and insight into the spiritual principalities and powers that exert influence and rulership over the Seven Mountains. It is as we gain this discernment that we can strategise with regard to "Invading" their territory and thus begin the process of "regime change".

Engagement in the "Invasion" stage weakens the hold of the principalities and powers and opens up the opportunity for the hearts and minds of the people to be influenced'.

Influence is the ability to effect change, and change is at the heart of the gospel. Apart from the instantaneous change from death to life at salvation, and apart from the immediacy of the transference from the kingdom of darkness into the Kingdom of God, the Christian life is one of continual change as the believer is changed from one degree of glory to another.

> *Therefore, I urge you, brothers, in view of God's mercy, to offer your bodies as living sacrifices, holy and pleasing to God – this is your spiritual act of worship. Do not conform any longer to the pattern of this world, but be transformed by the renewing of your mind. Then you will be able to test and approve what God's will is – his good, pleasing and perfect will.*

Romans 12:1-2

> *Now the Lord is the Spirit, and where the Spirit of the Lord is, there is freedom. And we, who with unveiled faces all reflect the Lord's glory, are being transformed into his likeness with ever-increasing glory, which comes from the Lord, who is the Spirit.*

2 Corinthians 3:17-18

Not only are Christians called to be in a continual process of transformation through the in-working of the word and of the Spirit, but Christians are also called to make a difference to the world in which they live.

The Great Commission is a command by Jesus, the head, to His body, to go and to make a difference in the world. The Kingdom of God is to be advanced as the church realises the responsibility it has to be "agents of change" and "people of influence."

Agents of Change and People of Influence

It is my contention that all Christians are called to be agents of change and people of influence. When Jesus called His disciples the *"light of the world"* and the *"salt of the earth"* He was expressing His plans for Christians to be not only seen from a distance, but also for them to be intimately engaged with the world around them.

With regard to the Seven Mountains, it is important for Christians to assume the responsibility of engagement. The reality is that all of us are engaged with the mountains in some way or another and we need to see that we are Kingdom ambassadors wherever, and wherever we find such engagement.

In recent years I have become increasingly aware of the enormous amount of influence even a small church can have on the surrounding community and beyond.

Influence in Risborough

When my wife, Jane, and I moved to Princes Risborough in 2000 we prayer walked the town asking the Holy Spirit to lead us to where we could make a connection. The fellowship was relatively small in those days, but we felt called to be "agents of change and people of influence". Our engagement began primarily with the young people of the town who tended to congregate aimlessly in the parks and dark corners of our beautiful little rural market town. For many in the town the youth seemed to be at the heart of every problem.

Our initial engagement was to purchase a small caravan and offer free shelter, warmth, hot drinks, bacon sandwiches, and a great deal of love and acceptance. The power of God's love and acceptance through us and our small team was a really powerful influence on these young lives, but to be brutally honest it was the aroma of sizzling bacon that really did the trick! A good fisherman selects appropriate bait!

Now more than ten years later that ministry has grown beyond all recognition and today we have access into many young lives on a weekly basis as we are welcomed into the schools and clubs in the town.

Recently we met up with one of our first contacts from the caravan ministry, now a very lovely young adult, and she was so appreciative of our input into her life in those crucial formative years.

There will be many reading this book who have been, or are today, or will be involved in these front line ministries and for you I thank God. Even what might seem small and insignificant at the time, can be a mighty force of influence in the years to come.

Be encouraged, look to see where you can be engaged and where you can exert Kingdom influence. It was through those early days of loving commitment to become "agents of change and people of influence" that God has graced us with ever increasing levels of influence in our local communities. May it ever increase and may we see the "Kingdom come and God's will be done".

Stage Five – Influence

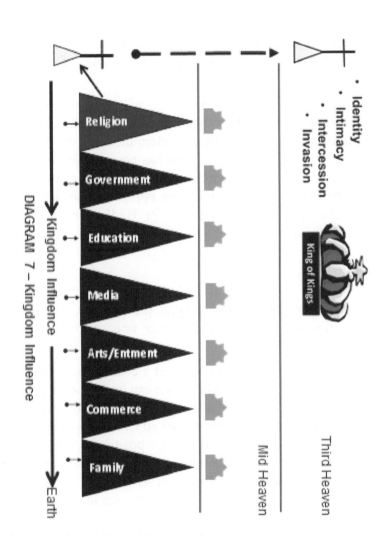

DIAGRAM 7 – Kingdom Influence

Kingdom Influence

Earth

- Religion
- Government
- Education
- Media
- Arts/Entment
- Commerce
- Family

Mid Heaven

Third Heaven

King of Kings

- Identity
- Intimacy
- Intercession
- Invasion

Explanation of Diagram 7

The final stage of the Fivefold Strategy is depicted in diagram 7. In this diagram it will be seen that the "True Church" has now been released on the horizontal plane to engage on the earth with the Seven Mountains as people of Kingdom Influence.

The effectiveness of this final stage will very much depend upon the progress in the other four. Certainly the ability for Christians to influence will be determined by the levels of "Intercession" and "Invasion" that has been carried out in the heavenly realms. The softening up of the demonic strongholds in the heavenly places reduces the opposition on the ground and opens up great opportunities for God's people to exert Kingdom Influence.

Multi-Level Influence

It is no doubt true that the higher the position held in any organisation the greater the influence one can exert on that organisation.

For example if the Prime Minister of a country is a committed Christian then the influence he or she can exert upon the affairs of state are far greater than a secretary in the local government offices. However it is important that all Christians seek to exert Kingdom influence wherever they are positioned. The story of Joseph gives us a good example of multi-level influence. The story is well worth reading in Genesis chapters 39 to 42. In brief, God was with Joseph even when he was in prison, and he was granted favour with the wardens. It was whilst he was incarcerated in the jail that he interpreted the dreams of the cupbearer to the king and also of the king's baker. These were important men, and although Pharaoh in fact hanged the baker, he restored the cup bearer to his exalted position.

Some two years later the Pharaoh had dreams but there was no one to interpret them. The cupbearer remembered Joseph and he was called to interpret the dreams of Pharaoh. Now the slave who had been an influence in the life of the cupbearer, was to be an influence to the ruling Pharaoh.

As a result of interpreting the dreams of Pharaoh, Joseph was placed in charge of the whole of Egypt. Truly Joseph had exerted Godly influence at the lowest level, but was now exalted to the highest. His influence changed the course of history for the Egyptians.

> *So Pharaoh said to Joseph, "I hereby put you in charge of the whole land of Egypt." Then Pharaoh took his signet ring from his finger and put it on Joseph's finger. He dressed him in robes of fine linen and put a gold chain around his neck. He had him ride in a chariot as his second-in-command, and men shouted before him, "Make way!" Thus he put him in charge of the whole land of Egypt.*

Genesis 41:41-43

This is a great story and shows what can happen when we release what we have, even though it may seem small at the time.

Another story that illustrates the importance of recognising the fact that influence can be exerted by anyone at any level is found in 2 Kings 5. It is the story of Naaman, a commander in the army of King Aram. He was a very important man, but was greatly afflicted with leprosy. Some of his soldiers had returned with a captured slave girl from Israel. It was this little slave girl that suggested Naaman seek healing from the prophet Elisha. Ultimately this is what happened, and so the insignificant slave girl was able to exert very significant influence far beyond her position in the household.

Influence in the Seven Mountains

It is so important for the church to appreciate that for the vast majority of our congregations their primary engagement with the world is in the work place. So often churches fail to see this and so most of the energy of church is expended in the continuance of church.

It is such a temptation for church leaders to encourage their best people to become leaders in the church, or even to take up "full time ministry". The fact is that all Christians should be engaged in full time ministry, 24/7, as we live for Jesus and for the Kingdom. We do not clock on and clock off as if our Christian life was some added extra.

To be truly significant a church will equip folk, not only for church based ministries, but also for workplace ministry. This equipping for the workplace will not only be specifically focussed on "how to evangelise your workplace", or "how to lead a colleague to Jesus", but will be toward equipping on a much broader basis.

How many of our churches gather together the members of the congregation who are top executives in major companies, and help them to address spiritual issues concerning their executive roles?

How many congregations pray for their members on a regular basis for the challenges that face them at work? How many intercessory groups do we have storming heaven for the banks, the factories, the shops, the schools?

Stage Five – Influence

It would be an interesting exercise to take a review of your congregation and see what each member is involved with during the week. In Chilterns Christian Fellowship we have a rich diversity of people, it is so exciting.

We have youngsters at school who are encouraged to live for Jesus and be agents of change where they are. We have folk away at university who we pray for on a regular basis. We have several members who are teachers and others involved in other aspects of the education system. We pray for them and see how we can help them to be salt and light where they are.

There are those who head up their own businesses, and in these times it is important that they are undergirded with prayer support and equipped to lead their workforce in Godly ways.

We also have some folk who are top executives in major companies in London. These people exert huge influence in their careers, not only in their personal witness, but also in making decisions with Kingdom integrity.

Within the congregation we are also blessed by having folk who exert a strong influence in the financial institutions of the City of London. These people speak boldly into these institutions promoting the principles of "ethical banking" and of righteous business. We have yet to directly engage with the mountain of Government although we continue to pray and intercede for all in office.

In the mix, we have missionary families, unemployed families, retired men and women, single parent families, and indeed some who are still trying to find out what life is all about. In addition we have folk in prison ministry, in care homes, local government, playgroups, family welfare, parenting classes and indeed much more. As such we engage in most of the Seven Mountains of Influence at many and varied levels.

These are not mentioned to promote the local church here in Princes Risborough. Indeed we realise that we are on a journey and in truth have only just begun. These are mentioned rather to encourage churches and church leaders to see the enormous potential for Kingdom Influence that perhaps is lying dormant in local churches. Apart from the Holy Spirit, our people are our greatest assets. It is not a question of "using them" but rather of equipping and releasing in order to transform the world around them.

Equipping the Saints

There is a powerful verse in Ephesians chapter four with regard to equipping the saints, that is the members of the true church.

> *It was he who gave some to be apostles, some to be prophets, some to be evangelists, and some to be pastors and teachers, to prepare God's people for works of service, so that the body of Christ may be built up until we all reach unity in the faith and in the knowledge of the Son of God and become mature, attaining to the whole measure of the fullness of Christ.*

Ephesians 4:11-13

I was "born again" in the late 1970s and at that time in the charismatic circles in which I found myself, there was a great emphasise on "Body Ministry" and "finding your gift". Whilst this was great and certainly generated rapid growth in those early days, it did rather shape my view of "equipping the saints". I became local church orientated, desiring to equip the saints for the work of the Sunday service! This tended to be somewhat introspective in terms of equipping. However we did have a passion to see folk come to faith in Christ, but in those days I had little understanding of the need to equip the church for the work outside the church.

Raising up Princes

Joseph was a prince in Egypt. He was not in his homeland but he was where God would have him at that time. He was God's man for that moment!

Joseph served in Potiphar's house but he did not serve Potiphar's god. Joseph remained loyal to his own God and as such received God's favour in the land.

I often pray for the men and women in my church who hold high office in places of significant influence that the same favour that was on Joseph will also be upon them. Joseph had prophetic insight and Godly wisdom, and it was these attributes that enabled him to be a man of great significance in the land of Egypt. Today, in our churches, we have men and women of great substance who carry such destiny on their lives. Even though the Seven Mountains may seem more like Egypt than the Kingdom, nonetheless, God's wisdom and anointing can make the difference.

Christian leaders today have a great responsibility to raise up such "Princes", and to be politically correct, "Princesses"! It is only God's people who are led by God's word, filled with God's Spirit, and blessed with God's favour. In truth the world systems need such leaders and the church is full of them.

To release our best to influence the world, is a major challenge to the church today, but one that is in keeping with the Great Commission of our leader.

> *All authority in heaven and on earth has been given to me. Therefore go and make disciples of all nations, baptizing them in the name of the Father and of the Son and of the Holy Spirit, and teaching them to obey everything I have commanded you. And surely I am with you always, to the very end of the age."*

> Matthew 28:18-20

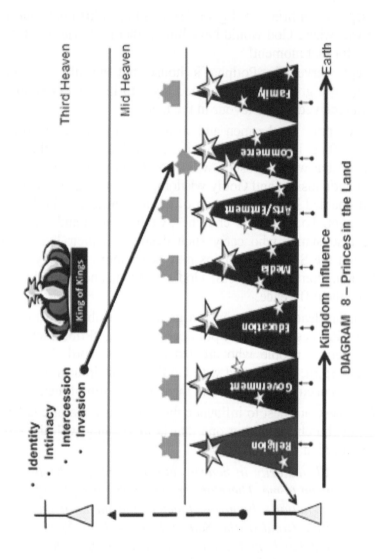

DIAGRAM 8 – Princes in the Land

Stage Five – Influence

Explaining Diagram **8**

Diagram 8 illustrates how raising up "Princes in the Land" and seeing them established in positions of authority can exert significant influence within each of the Seven Mountains.

As these Princes, and Princesses, represented by stars, are raised up within the mountains then their effectiveness as "Agents of Change and People of Influence" increases. Righteous and ethical decisions in top management can change not only the environment within the mountain but also will weaken the stronghold over it. The principle of Romans 6:16 is activated and the power of the spiritual bondage is broken.

The different size stars represent the different levels of influence within the mountain. As Christians begin to engage with the mountain they will enter at a lower level of influence than someone who has been involved for a longer period. As they progress, and with God's favour they will, they will be able to exert more Kingdom influence in decision making and in shaping the ethics by which the mountain operates.

Focus on the Mountain of Commerce

For the ease of explanation we will take just one mountain to show the principle at work. The Mountain of Commerce is the choice. This mountain has been "loaded" with Kingdom influence as individual Christians engage at various levels within the mountain. At each level, whether it be at ground level, or the heady heights of the Board Room every Christian is both "salt and light" in the establishment.

As their engagement within the practicalities of the mountain is supported by the intercession and invasion tactics of others standing with them in the place of spiritual authority, the controlling principality and power is weakened, and in this case, dethroned as represented by the fallen crown.

This may seem somewhat simplistic in principle but effective Kingdom influence does not need to be complicated nor indeed mystical and super spiritual. Effective Kingdom influence just needs Christians to be real and to be focussed.

A word to Pastors and Church Leaders

Let the experts be the experts! However well-meaning pastors and church leaders may be, the sad reality is that we do not know everything about everything! Now this may come as a shock to some folk, especially pastors and church leaders, however it is true.

The role of pastors and church leaders in God's Fivefold Strategy is not, repeat not, to expect to engage with the different mountains as some sort of all embracing expert, but rather to equip and support the folk in our churches who are already professional experts in their own mountain.

It may well be that by praying with the individuals the Holy Spirit may give the pastor or church leaders some prophetic insight into specific situations within the professional machinery of the mountain that will enable the "expert" to make Kingdom decisions. This has happened on a number of occasions as I have prayed with my own church members. The Holy Spirit has given prophetic insight into areas of expertise that has been way outside of my own knowledge, but that has shaped professional decision making and enabled the Kingdom to advance.

Pastors and church leaders have the most privileged and exciting of roles within God's Fivefold Strategy, and that is of caring for, equipping, empowering and then releasing the most potent force on the planet; spirit filled Kingdom people who will be "Agents of Change and People of Influence".

26

Finally – Be Intentional

Finally – "Be Intentional". The encouraging reality is that most of what has been written in this book, is in fact already happening to some degree or another, but often by accident rather than intention.

The aim of this book has been to gather together the various strands of current activities regarding the Kingdom of God. It has then attempted to bring a cohesive overview and workable strategy to assist with the desire of many to engage meaningfully with the world around us.

At each stage in the Fivefold Strategy there is a need to be "Intentional". To fully appreciate the powerful realities of the believer's true identity in Christ, is to be raised up from the constraints of mediocrity into the glorious inheritance of the true church. Intentionality at this stage is to choose to live as such and not to be limited by the experience of history, but to rise up and to grasp the fullness of our destiny in Christ.

It is from that place of understanding "Identity" that we can truly appreciate the restoration of "Intimacy" with Father God. Intimacy with Father God is a life changing revelation and a glorious reality. God will always be the Almighty Transcendent One, the Creator of Heaven and Earth, but now He is also the One who draws us to Himself in that place of Intimacy where we can hear the whispers of that "still small voice". Intentionality here is to make the time to be with Him, and to make the main thing the main thing.

As the heartbeat of God is heard in that secret place of "Intimacy", so our heart becomes moved by what moves Him. Intercession is that passionate heart cry of the believer who is both intimately in touch with God and also with the people and the issues of the world. Intentionality in intercession is to take that place between the problem and the provider until the provision is realised. Intentionality in intercession is the dogged determination to stay engaged until the answer comes.

With regard to the Fivefold Strategy, intercession is connecting with the people in the mountains and supporting them in prayer. It is the upholding of the believers as they face the decisions that could change the very nature of the mountain itself.

Through the "connectedness" of intercession the believer will gain great spiritual insight into the principalities and powers that exert spiritual control over the mountains. A full appreciation of relative strengths is one of the first principles of strategic planning. In fully understanding our own identity in Christ and the relative positioning of the ruling principalities and powers we can begin to formulate the strategy for "Invasion".

Intentionality at the Invasion Stage is to identify the spiritual forces through observation, spiritual insight and research, and then to determine the will of God in that given situation. Once the will of God is known, then prophetic declaration is made as ambassadors of the Kingdom, declaring "this is the will of God", and commanding the spiritual powers to submit to it.

Finally – Be Intentional

There may be a need for those "Princes and Princesses" in places of authority in the mountains to be intentional and take their place in "Identification confession". This can only be accomplished by Christians who are engaged in the mountain for which repentance is required.

Finally, we have 'Influence'. In truth, every person exerts influence just by the way they inter-act with others, but not all influence is good. Being 'Intentional' with Kingdom influence is first to live "full" and then to "overflow" with the presence, with the Spirit, and with the love of God.

All Christians everywhere, not only those in exalted positions in the mountains, have great potential to release Kingdom influence. It starts in the home and in the family. It widens to friends, relatives and neighbours. Local community groups can be greatly influenced by the presence of Christians, as indeed can schools at all levels, as Christians engage with "intentionality" as parents and as school governors.

For those "Princes and Princesses" in exalted positions of influence in the mountains, "intentionality" means that they choose to be true to the ethics and values of the Kingdom when making decisions and setting policies. This may indeed present some challenges of expediency, but they should trust the God who exalted them, to be the God who will honour them.

And finally, for all believers everywhere who seek the will of God who desire earnestly that the "Kingdom of God come on earth as it is in heaven", let the words of the Apostle Paul to the church at Ephesus be both an instruction and an encouragement.

> *Finally, be strong in the Lord and in his mighty power. Put on the full armour of God so that you can take your stand against the devil's schemes. For our struggle is not against flesh*

and blood, but against the rulers, against the authorities, against the powers of this dark world and against the spiritual forces of evil in the heavenly realms.

Therefore put on the full armour of God, so that when the day of evil comes, you may be able to stand your ground, and after you have done everything, to stand. Stand firm then, with the belt of truth buckled around your waist, with the breastplate of righteousness in place, and with your feet fitted with the readiness that comes from the gospel of peace.

In addition to all this, take up the shield of faith, with which you can extinguish all the flaming arrows of the evil one. Take the helmet of salvation and the sword of the Spirit, which is the word of God. And pray in the Spirit on all occasions with all kinds of prayers and requests. With this in mind, be alert and always keep on praying for all the saints.

Ephesians 6:10-18

Dear Heavenly Father, may your will be done, and your Kingdom come, on earth as it is in heaven. Amen.

Kingdom and Culture

Kingdom and Culture

An environmentally friendly book printed and bound in England by www.printondemand-worldwide.com

This book is made of chain-of-custody materials; FSC materials for the cover and PEFC materials for the text pages.